SIMPLY
DELICIOUS

Wine

RECIPES

Country

"I enjoy cooking with wine, sometimes I even put it in the food."

—JULIA CHILD
(1912–2004)

SIMPLY
DELICIOUS

Wine Country Recipes

ROBIN GOLDSTEIN

Photography by Tenley Allensworth Fohl

Published by

M27 Editions LLC
3030 State Street
Santa Barbara, California 93105
PHONE (805) 563-0099
FAX (805) 563-2070
EMAIL publish@m27editions.com
WEB www.m27editions.com

For cooking classes, workshops and retreats, and merchandise:
WEB privatechefrobin.com
atasteofCA.com
EMAIL privatechefrobin@gmail.com

Simply Delicious Wine Country Recipes
by Robin Goldstein
Photography by Tenley Allensworth Fohl

First Printing

ISBN: 9780996863537
Library of Congress Control Number: 2017910958

Design and Production by Media 27, Inc., Santa Barbara, California

WWW.MEDIA27.COM

Printed in China

dedication

For my daughter, Chiya Bella

The greatest gift I have been given, by far, is you,
always inspiring me to be patient and understanding
and to set things aside and just be.

Best of all, I am my most authentic self when I am with you.

I love you, my sweetheart, with all my heart,
all my soul, and all my world!

contents

INTRODUCTION

A VISIT TO WINE COUNTRY revives the soul and soothes the senses. It's no accident that my favorite places—Spain, France, Italy, Greece, the Middle East, and California, my home for the past 30 years—are known for their marriage of food and wine. These parts of the world, blessed with a Mediterranean climate, have inspired "wine country cooking"—a simple, updated way of preparing and eating food that celebrates seasonal fruit and produce, farm-raised meats, fresh fish and seafood—all paired with favorite wines.

There's no mystery to matching wine and food, as long as you are enjoying yourself while you're eating and drinking. That basic level is where great meals begin; that elementary pleasure is a springboard to exploring the vast and varied world of wine country cuisine.

I've had a connection with the kitchen and food as far back as I can remember. I have vivid memories of my grandmother making strudel by hand, rolling the dough as thin as paper on her marble table for the restaurant she and my grandfather owned. My father owned and managed restaurants as well. But my true culinary epiphany came at age 14, when I started doctoring the meals my mom made. She worked full-time, and with 3 young girls at home, she just quickly threw things together with little sense of adventure or much emphasis on flavor. I remember experimenting with spices, adding a pinch of this or that from the drawer of herbs, and getting rave reviews from my family. Their reaction was a powerful motivation. Cooking for me was everything!

I'd come home from school to watch a sappy soap opera on TV until Julia Child came on, followed by Graham Kerr, the Galloping Gourmet. I wasn't reading the next Nancy Drew adventure; I was pouring over my mother's copies of *Gourmet*. That magazine opened the world of food for many of us. We were inspired by the exotic ingredients from faraway lands. Those images and words shaped my aspirations and piqued my desire to travel.

Later, I honed my cooking skills at the Culinary Institute of America in New York. There, I learned how to hold and sharpen a knife, bake, carve, julienne, and chiffonade with finesse, dress salads with ease, and set a classic table. Promptly after culinary school, I drove across

"Everyone has been made for some particular work, and
the desire for that work has been put in every heart."

—RUMI

the country to California and started my career in the
food industry. I cooked privately for high-profile clients.
I even worked as chef to a Grammy award-winning singer;
living and traveling on a tour bus for a year. Later, when
I owned and operated my catering and private chef
business, I would focus on individual clients and their
entertaining needs.

Someone once said, "If you do what you love, you'll never
work a day in your life." I truly believe that. I have created
my life's work, pursued a career, and grown a business
around cooking. I am very passionate about what I do
every day.

Of course, preparing and cooking food takes time. Some
people think they're far too busy to imagine cooking a
meal, or they may not have confidence in the kitchen.
To them, I say that the secret lies in realizing that although
cooking is a creative endeavor, it's also a process. Making
a recipe means reading the recipe through to the end,
gathering all the ingredients, and then following through. When I cook,
I stay calm and collected. One thing that helps tremendously is
writing out a prep list the day before, so I can keep track of everything
I must do to lead to the finished meal. That's something everyone
can do.

Above all, I want to inspire people who say they can't cook. I can
assure you that with these wine country recipes, you won't have
to spend hours upon hours in the kitchen to create a great dish.
Sharing food—even the simplest of homemade meals—with friends
and family is one of the most rewarding and sociable forms of
communication.

For me, cooking has remained a joyful activity over the years. With
this book, I hope you can share in that pleasure, as well.

Chef Robin

WINE COUNTRY INSPIRATIONS

ONE OF THE FIRST TIMES I cooked in the Santa Ynez Valley, I was super excited to work for a group of vacationing clients. They were celebrating a birthday and wanted to stretch the meal out with several courses and paired wines that they had found on their wine-tasting outing. I had given the host many suggestions to choose from, but he chose everything! It was hilarious. He must have been quite hungry while reviewing the menu, or perhaps the surroundings really whetted his appetite.

It's true that the Santa Ynez Valley, which sprawls over 300,000 acres, is a special place—and that starts with the geography. The mountains here are part of the Transverse Ranges. They run east-west, instead of the more common north-south orientation, and that has a dramatic affect on the climate, which is Mediterranean—reminiscent of Portugal, Spain, France, Italy, and Greece. Summers can be very hot and extremely dry; winters are mild and wet. There are also many micro-climates that encourage the successful growing of high-quality fruit from a wide range of wine grape varieties. Over the last 50 years, winegrowers have responded by planting Chardonnay, Pinot Noir, Syrah, Sauvignon Blanc, Pinot Grigio, Cabernet Sauvignon, and Viognier, among many others. (See below for a full list of varietals grown here.)

Today the Santa Ynez Valley features both small privately-owned boutique wineries and large estate vineyards, many of which are family-owned and operated. With four distinct American Viticultural Areas (AVAs)—six in all of Santa Barbara County—more than one million cases of wine are produced annually. The rural flavor of the area provides a welcoming backdrop for visitors who come to taste world-class wines in an unpretentious, friendly atmosphere where it's not unusual to end up chatting with the winemaker or owner—either at the winery or in-town tasting rooms.

Of course, wine enhances food, and food enhances wine, so the availability of these great varietals turns any chef's thoughts to what to serve with them. A lot has been written about

perfect wine pairings. But I believe you don't have to be a sommelier to pair food and wine, and you certainly don't need a degree or an app on your phone. One school of thought is that you can drink whatever you want to drink with whatever you feel like eating, and you'll still have a pretty great experience. In fact, I've found that you can have a particular wine that you love and have had many times, but when you pair it with different foods, it tastes totally different.

The dishes in this book were broadly inspired by the bounty of Santa Ynez Valley's wine country, but they are meant to be enjoyed anywhere and everywhere. The key is to start with healthful and high-quality ingredients. You will also discover that none of my recipes are too complicated, and all of them work. It was Julia Child who said, "Cooking well doesn't mean cooking fancy." It gives me freedom when I'm writing recipes to know that when I suggest what's in season, I can also suggest alternative options that reflect my creative flavor combinations. Many of the dishes in this cookbook tell a story or relate to a personal memory, and I've included things I loved as a child and that I have continued to love as an adult.

The recipes that follow generally flow from appetizers to dessert and range from lighter entrées to more substantial ones. I've also included sections on dishes that rely on cheeses and grapes because...well, why not? These are ingredients that seem to epitomize the delights of wine country cuisine, and it's fun to showcase myriad ways to enjoy them.

"The Perfect Bites" section is based on tasty, tiny hors d'oeuvres—delectable morsels, like **Crab Beignets**, which are delicious fried tidbits that will wow your guests without adding too many calories. And in the height of the summer season, there's nothing like **Prosciutto-Wrapped Grilled Peaches**. You lightly grill them to bring out the saltiness in the ham. My mouth waters just thinking about it!

The ideal wine to serve with these starters is something cold with high acidity. White varietals fit these requirements perfectly; think about a well-chilled dry sparkling wine or white wine—Pinot Grigio or Grüner Veltliner, as an

example. For spicy or fried foods, any aromatic white wine, like Sauvignon Blanc, can be an impressive pairing. A dry crisp, bright Riesling is also great with cheeses and richer foods, particularly blue cheese. Light and refreshing rosé wines—with hues that range from salmon and copper to cranberry—have become a summer favorite.

"A Taste of Cheese" begins with the **Ultimate Cheese Board**, which I consider a wonderful way to kick off any gathering of friends. The choice of cheeses will be up to you, but I've included some tasty accompaniments that will add color and crunch to the table. How satisfying it is to present homemade condiments. **Pickled Grapes**, for example, are easy to make and definitely worth the effort, along with hand-rolled **Wine Country Biscuits** and **Parmesan Cheese Straws**. **Strawberry–Black Pepper Jam** and **Homemade Mustard** will have your friends thinking you have labored for days.

"With White Wine" is a collection of soups and lighter fare that pair well with, yes, the white varietals. The light, delicate flavors of these wines can sometimes be overwhelmed by spicy dishes, but when you get the balance of flavors right, the subtle flavors of the food will emerge. Because of the richness of Chardonnay, that wine does nicely with fatty-creamy foods, goat cheese, cream sauces, white meats, and many seafood dishes. It's great with the **Roasted Corn and Crab Chowder**, for example, and pairs well with crispy **Parmesan-Crusted Chicken**. A perfumy Viognier or Grenache Blanc—typically full-bodied, low-acid wines with hints of almonds, white peach, and ripe pear—complement the citrus notes in the **Good Friday Fish with Crispy Dill**.

"Grapes Notes" highlights an array of dishes that make use of the fruit of the vine, including a couple of starters and a knockout **Spanish Grape Tart** for dessert. The entrées in this section, like those in "With Red Wine," stand up particularly well to a medium or full-bodied red wine. The robust flavors of lamb and beef

work better with something younger and more fruit driven. For **Grilled Lamb Medallions with Grape Glaze** or **Lamb Shanks with Figs and Rosemary**, Pinot Noir or Sangiovese are favorites. With **Syrah-Braised Short Ribs** or a grilled rib-eye steak with **Chimichurri**, a jammy Zinfandel, tannin-rich Cabernet, or powerful inky Syrah would be classic matches.

Dessert lovers will relish "Delicious Endings," which incorporates the luscious tastes of fresh produce. For these, think of wines that are less sweet and lower in tannins, especially when serving a dish that uses berries and grapes. Pinot Noir, Sangiovese, and Tempranillo play well with the fresh **Grape Crostata with Ricotta Cream** and other berry-filled fruit desserts. Viognier and Grenache Blanc pair nicely with the **Autumn Fruit Compote with Lemon Panna Cotta** and would be amazing with the **Pan-Roasted Peaches with Lavender and Rosemary**. Or, of course, you could simply finish off your meal with **Dark Chocolate Wine Truffles**. Enjoy!

——— VARIETALS GROWN IN THE SANTA YNEZ VALLEY/SANTA BARBARA COUNTY ———

Albariño	**Grenache**	Muscat Canelli	**Sangiovese**
Arneis	Grenache Blanc	Nebbiolo	**Sauvignon Blanc**
Cabernet Franc	Grenache Gris	Negrette	Sémillon
Cabernet Sauvignon	Lagrein	Petit Verdot	**Syrah**
Carignane	Malbec	**Pinot Grigio/Gris**	Tempranillo
Chardonnay	Malvasia	**Pinot Noir**	Valdepenas
Cinsault	Marsanne	Primitivo	Tocai Friulano
Counoise	**Merlot**	Riesling	**Viognier**
Gewurztraminer	Mourvedre	Roussanne	Zinfandel

*Wines shown in bold are highest in production.

WINEMAKING IN SANTA BARBARA

1782 — Father Junípero Serra planted Mission vine cuttings in what is now the Milpas District of Santa Barbara

1804 — Adobe winery constructed in Goleta

1884 — Justinian Caire imported grape slips (*vitis vinifera*) from France and planted a 150-acre vineyard on Santa Cruz Island

1933 — 45 separate vineyards encompassing 260 acres of land are cultivated to wine grapes; Prohibition repealed

1960s — First commercial vineyard planted by Uriel Nielsen and Bill De Mattei in the Tepusquet region of Santa Maria Valley

1962 — Pierre Lafond opens Santa Barbara Winery, the first winery since Prohibition

1970s — Vineyard expansion by viticultural pioneers

1980s — Local wineries—both large premium commercial wineries and smaller artisan operations—developed

1981, 1983 — Santa Maria Valley and Santa Ynez Valley recognized as official AVAs

Santa Barbara County has a history of growing grapes and winemaking that stretches back more than 200 years, to the Mission Era of early California. The 1960s inaugurated today's interest in winemaking here, and Santa Barbara County continues to combine traditional, hand-made techniques with the latest cutting-edge innovations.

Santa Barbara County Vintners Association formed

Grape and wine sales increase, making the wine industry Santa Barbara County's largest agricultural sector

Sta. Rita Hills granted official AVA status

Happy Canyon of Santa Barbara granted official AVA status

Los Olivos District granted official AVA status

1983   1990s   1992-1996   1999   2001   2004   2009   2013   2015

Explosive growth to 10,000-plus acres of premium wine grapes

39,200 tons of wine grapes crushed from 16,500 acres of vineyards. Locally, 50+ wineries produced 71,000 cases of wine

Sideways movie brings attention and increased tourism

Ballard Canyon granted official AVA status

Wine Facts

In ancient Greece, a dinner host would take the first sip of wine to assure guests that the drink was not poisoned, hence the phrase drinking to one's health.

In ancient Rome, toasting started when the Romans—continuing the Greek tradition—started dropping a piece of toasted bread into the glass to temper the wine's acidity or any undesirable tastes.

The Vikings called America "Vinland" (wine-land) for the profusion of native grape vines they found there around 1,000 A.D.

Red wines are red because fermentation extracts color from the grape skins. White wines are not fermented with the skins present.

The smell of young wine is called "aroma," while a more mature wine offers a more subtle "bouquet."

Since wine tasting is essentially wine smelling, women tend to be better wine testers because women, particularly of reproductive age, have a better sense of smell than men.

Women are more susceptible to the effects of wine than men, partly because they have fewer enzymes in the lining of their stomachs, which are needed to metabolize alcohol efficiently.

An Italian study argues that women who drink two glasses of wine a day have better sex than those who don't drink at all!

The vintage year isn't necessarily the year wine is bottled, because some wines may not be bottled the same year the grapes are picked. Typically, a vintage wine is a product of a single year's harvest. A nonvintage wine is a blend of wines from two or more years.

California is the fourth-largest wine producer in the world, after France, Italy, and Spain.

Wine grapes rank number one among the world's fruit crops in terms of acres planted.

"Wine gives great pleasure,
and every pleasure is
of itself a good."

—SAMUEL JOHNSON (1709–1984)
BOSWELL'S *LIFE OF JOHNSON*

perfect bites

Mix and mingle with your guests while snacking on these perfect bites. These fantastic little appetizers take next to no time or effort and only require five ingredients more or less—simple morsels that pair perfectly with wine.

PERFECT BITES

A single bite-size hors d'oeuvre, or *amuse bouche* (literally meaning "to amuse the mouth"), is an ideal way to start any soiree or dinner party. The purpose of these starters is to complement the wine and give your guests something to do while they wait for the main event!

CHÈVRE-STUFFED DATES WITH PECANS

MAKES 2 DOZEN AND MORE

24 Medjool dates
    (or any large date), pitted

1 small log of fresh chèvre
    (goat cheese)

24 pecan halves

12 strips of bacon,
    cut in half crosswise

Toothpicks

Preheat the oven to 375°F. Split the dates to remove the pits. Take a small chunk of chèvre and push it into the date using a pecan half. Don't overfill the dates or you will end up with a messy oven. Wrap each filled date in a half slice of bacon and secure with a toothpick. Place on a baking pan. (I use a silicone pad or line the pan with foil for easy cleanup; do not use parchment here as it can easily burn.) Bake for 20–30 minutes, or until the bacon is fully crisp. Remove from the pan onto a paper towel to drain. Plate and serve after cooling for a few minutes.

SPICED OIL-CURED OLIVES

MAKES 2 CUPS

2 cups Kalamata or your
    favorite olives

2 teaspoons chile flakes

1 teaspoon ground cumin

Zest and juice of 1 large lemon

½ cup extra virgin olive oil

Combine all ingredients in a bowl. Marinate at room temperature for an hour or so to infuse the flavors, then store in a covered glass Mason jar in the refrigerator until ready to use. Make sure the olives are immersed in the olive oil, and they will keep for several weeks.

BLUE CHEESE BITES

MAKES 2 DOZEN AND MORE

8 ounces cream cheese,
    softened

8 ounces creamy blue cheese,
    room temperature

2 tablespoons chopped dates
    or other dried fruit

1 cup chopped toasted pecans
    or walnuts, divided in half

1 teaspoon sea salt

Freshly ground pepper

In a small bowl, mix the softened cream cheese, blue cheese, dates or dried fruit, and half of the chopped nuts, until completely combined. Season with salt and a few grinds of pepper. Refrigerate for 30 minutes, until slightly firm and workable.

Roll the cheese into small bite-size balls and roll in the chopped nuts to coat.

Place on your serving plate and enjoy!

USING GRAPE LEAVES

Using grape leaves with foods is unusual in the United States, even though it is common in the Middle East, and dates all the way back to the days of Alexander the Great. Dolmades—grape leaves stuffed with rice and pine nuts and sometimes sweetened with currants—are a classic Greek appetizer. Authentic Egyptian stuffed grape leaves, similar to cabbage rolls, are filled with lamb or beef and fragrantly spiced by cloves, allspice, ginger, cardamom, and cinnamon. Grape leaves can swaddle a whole trout to be grilled, envelop chicken filled with spinach, wrap small pieces of cheese to be fried or served chilled with lemon, or be used in the Fried Stuffed Grape Leaves recipe here.

You can prepare your own grape leaves: They are best picked in late spring and early summer, from late April through June, while they are still tender and before any grapes are visible on the vines. It is also important to pick the leaves early in the day and from unsprayed vines, as some sprays are toxic.

To prepare for culinary uses

~ Cut off the stems with a sharp knife or scissors; then rinse the grape leaves thoroughly in cold water and drain.

~ Blanch the grape leaves before using. If you plan on using the leaves within a few days, soak them in very hot water for 15 minutes to soften them.

~ If you want to keep the leaves longer, blanch them in a sea-salt brine until they are soft. The brine recipe is simple:

Bring 4 cups water and 1 cup sea salt to a boil. Add the grape leaves, approximately one dozen at a time, stirring them into the water. Quickly remove the grape leaves and plunge them into ice water. Drain and dry the leaves with paper towels. This step helps set the color in the leaves.

~ Store the grape leaves between layers of paper towels in airtight resealable plastic bags and freeze until ready to use. Frozen grape leaves last no more than 3 months in the freezer. Use them as soon as you thaw them as they do not keep well after freezing.

To use bottled grape leaves

~ To prepare bottled grape leaves, rinse them well under cold water to remove the brine. Place the leaves in a colander to drain and hold until ready to use.

chef's note
Do not throw away any torn or damaged leaves, as they can be used to patch holes in other leaves

FRIED STUFFED GRAPE LEAVES

These minuscule bites of joy require a little bit of work but make wonderful appetizers. Perhaps my favorite thing to do with grape leaves is to stuffed them with feta cheese, olives and pistachios, but I have also had success stuffing them with figs and gorgonzola cheese.

MAKES 2 DOZEN

24 grape leaves, fresh or from a jar—drained and rinsed

¼ cup green olives, chopped fine

¼ cup Kalamata olives, chopped fine

¼ cup sun-dried tomatoes, chopped fine

2 garlic cloves, minced

2 cups feta cheese, crumbled

⅓ cup pistachio nuts, chopped fine

¼ cup fresh basil leaves, chopped fine

Freshly ground pepper and sea salt

Extra virgin olive oil

Lemon wedges

In a bowl, mix the olives, sun-dried tomatoes, garlic, feta cheese, chopped pistachio nuts, and basil, with ¼ teaspoon salt and a few grinds of pepper. Remember the olives are salted, and both the sun-dried tomatoes and feta cheese can be salty too. (All of these ingredients can easily be combined by pulsing in a food processor.)

To stuff the leaves, start with your largest leaves and arrange 6 on a board in front of you. Take the leaves and carefully spread out with the veins facing upward to you (shiny side down). If the leaf is torn or has a hole in it, take a reserved damaged leaf and use it as a patch; place the leaf over the hole.

Place a heaped tablespoonful of the olive and feta mixture in the center near the stem end of the leaf (the amount of stuffing will depend on the size of the leaves). Press the stuffing into a small sausage-like shape. Fold the stem end of the leaf over the filling, then fold both sides toward the middle, and then roll up into a cigar shape. The rolls should be about 2 inches long and ½-inch thick. Squeeze lightly in the palm of your hand to secure the rolls. Repeat with the remaining grape leaves and filling.

Over medium heat, in a nonstick ceramic skillet when it's good and hot, add 2 tablespoons of olive oil. Wait a few seconds for the oil to heat, put in the dolmas with the last fold downward, to hold it in place. Fry until browned but not blackened, flip, and brown the other side. Transfer the fried grape rolls to a serving dish.

Serve warm with lemon.

CRAB BEIGNETS

These savory fritters of crispy crab morsels in a light batter are simple to prepare and perfect for entertaining. Oh, and did I mention totally addictive? Once your guests try a bite, they won't be able to stop.

MAKES 2 DOZEN OR MORE

3 eggs

2 tablespoons Old Bay Seasoning

8 ounces lump crab meat

½ cup unbleached white flour

¼ cup cornstarch

1 teaspoon baking powder

1 teaspoon sea salt

1 cup beer

¼ cup green bell pepper, diced

½ cup green onion, diced

1 tablespoon garlic, minced

1 teaspoon chopped jalapeño or serrano chiles, optional

2 quarts vegetable oil

In a large mixing bowl, whisk the eggs with the Old Bay Seasoning until frothy and add the crab meat to the egg mixture.

In another large bowl, whisk together the flour, cornstarch, baking powder, and salt. Gradually whisk in the beer, just to blend (batter will be thick). Fold into the crab mixture, along with the diced green pepper, onion, garlic, and chile, if using.

Heat the oil in a heavy-bottomed saucepan to 350°F, using a thermometer to check the temperature.

Divide the fritter mixture into 24 small portions—a heaping tablespoon or smaller for mini bites—and fry 6–8 fritters at a time in the hot oil, maintaining the temperature until the fritters turn golden brown, 3–4 minutes for each batch. Remove with a slotted spoon onto a paper towel to drain.

Plate and serve after cooling for a few minutes.

chef's note
These fritters are best served warm just after frying with a homemade aioli, tartar sauce, or cocktail sauce, and fresh lemon wedges.

COUNTRY-STYLE CHICKEN LIVER SPREAD

This Tuscan favorite, luscious and rustic, reflects its well-known peasant roots in a cuisine in which nothing was thrown away. *Crostini di fegatini* is featured on the menu of literally every trattoria in Tuscany, served as a traditional starter.

SERVES 4–6

4 tablespoons butter

4 tablespoons extra virgin olive oil

2 medium-size red onions, sliced thin

2 tablespoons light brown sugar

1 pound fresh chicken livers, rinsed

2 garlic cloves, chopped fine

1 tablespoon chopped fresh thyme

2 tablespoons white wine or sherry

Freshly ground pepper and sea salt

In a large skillet on medium-high heat, fry the onions in 2 tablespoons butter and 2 tablespoons olive oil until they begin to brown. Add the brown sugar and ½ teaspoon salt and stir together to dissolve the sugar. Adjust the heat to simmer for 5 minutes or so, stirring occasionally, until the mixture is browned and caramelized. Set aside.

Separately, melt 2 tablespoons butter with 2 tablespoons olive oil in a large skillet, add the chicken livers and garlic, and sauté until the chicken livers are browned and thoroughly cooked through. Season with ½ teaspoon salt and a few grinds of pepper, add the white wine or sherry, scraping up any browned bits on the bottom of the pan. Stir the onions into the liver. This can be processed in the food processor, pulsing to make a rustic country spread, or process a bit more to make a smooth spread. Taste and add more salt, as needed.

Spoon into a serving dish or lidded glass jar and serve with toast or crostini as an accompaniment to your cheese board.

PROSCIUTTO-WRAPPED GRILLED PEACHES

Salty cured ham amps up the sweetness of local peaches at their peak freshness, and the thick balsamic drizzle adds to the contrast of tart and sweet. Try this recipe with nectarines, white peaches, apricots, or even pears.

MAKES 2 DOZEN PIECES

12 prosciutto slices,
   cut in half lengthwise

24 large basil leaves, plus more
   for garnish

3 firm peaches, each cut into
   8 wedges

1 cup extra virgin olive oil

¼ teaspoon sea salt

Freshly ground pepper

½ cup balsamic glaze,
   store bought or homemade

Lay the prosciutto slices on a board with a large basil leaf on one end.

Place a wedge of fruit on the basil and wrap in the prosciutto slice.

Mix the olive oil with salt and a few grinds of pepper, brush each very lightly, and grill on a hot grill to sear the meat—the crustier the better.

Arrange the wrapped peaches on a serving tray and drizzle with balsamic glaze and any leftover seasoned olive oil.

Garnish with freshly torn basil leaves.

GRILLED OYSTERS WITH SRIRACHA-LIME BUTTER

When grilled oysters are jazzed up with a lime butter, the heat of Sriracha doesn't cling to your mouth, and the fresh lime juice gives it a nice acidity. Set them on a tray spread with coarse sea salt to hold the shells, or serve on individual plates with extra lemon and lime. Oyster plates can often be found in vintage stores and flea markets around town to create an impressive presentation.

FOR 1 DOZEN OYSTERS

½ cup salted butter, softened

2 teaspoons Sriracha

2 teaspoons shallots, minced fine

1 tablespoon lime juice

2 teaspoons cilantro, chopped

Oysters on the half shell

Lime or lemon wedges and Sriracha-lime salt for garnish

Mix the butter with the Sriracha, shallots, lime juice, and cilantro and set aside until ready to use.

Just before serving, heat a grill (or a broiler) until very hot.

Set up your oysters on a baking sheet pan, then top each oyster with a small dollop of Sriracha butter. Place the whole pan on the grill (or under broiler) for 3–4 minutes only and serve right away; be careful as the shells are very hot.

Finish off the oysters with a sprinkling of Sriracha-lime salt.

SRIRACHA-LIME SALT

Extremely versatile, infused salts will intensify the flavor in any recipe. I love making different infusions and sharing them with friends and clients as great homemade gifts. Use about 1 teaspoon spice or dried herb to ¼ cup of salt, but with fresh citrus zest or fresh herbs you can be more generous. Remember, there are many different types of salts to use.

½ cup sea salt

1 tablespoon Sriracha

Zest of 1 lime, grated

Combine all the ingredients in a bowl. Stir until salt has completely absorbed the flavorings and changed color. Pour onto a parchment paper–lined baking sheet and allow to air dry for 2 days, stirring frequently. You can also "heat dry" the salt in the oven at 170°F or lower for 2 hours, stirring frequently. Once dry, store in an airtight container. Use within 3 months.

OYSTER MUSHROOM ROCKEFELLER

I love the play on words: Oyster mushrooms stand in for oysters in this Rockefeller, a take on the classic oysters Rockefeller with wild mushrooms. Besides that, they taste really great, and they are fun to eat on the artichoke leaves that stand in for oyster shells.

——— MAKES FILLING FOR 2 DOZEN ARTICHOKE LEAVES ———

1 tablespoon extra virgin olive oil

12 oyster mushrooms,
   trimmed, sliced thin

¼ cup white onion, chopped fine

1 tablespoon garlic, minced

Freshly ground pepper
   and sea salt

2 tablespoons white wine

½ cup cooked spinach

½ cup artichoke hearts,
   chopped fine

½ cup Parmesan cheese, grated

4 tablespoons bread crumbs

1 tablespoon parsley,
   chopped fine

Pinch of chile flakes

2 whole artichokes, cooked,
   (pick 24 larger outer leaves
   for use)

Fresh lemon wedges

Heat a large sauté pan over medium heat. Sauté the mushrooms in the olive oil with the onion and garlic for 2–3 minutes. Add ½ teaspoon salt and the white wine, and continue cooking until the edges of the mushrooms are lightly browned. Remove the mushrooms to a medium bowl and stir the cooked spinach and chopped artichoke hearts into the mushroom mixture.

Mix the Parmesan with the bread crumbs and chopped parsley in a separate bowl, and season with ½ teaspoon salt, ¼ teaspoon pepper, and a pinch or two of chile flakes.

Preheat the broiler on high.

Place the 24 cooked artichoke leaves on a baking pan an inch apart and top each one with a heaping tablespoon of the mushroom-spinach mixture. Sprinkle each leaf with ½ tablespoon of the Parmesan mixture and drizzle with olive oil. Broil for 2–3 minutes or until browned. Serve warm as a passed appetizer, or place several on a plate as a first course.

Serve with fresh lemon.

WHITE BEAN AND SPINACH FLATBREAD

Flatbreads are designed to impress, yet they are easy to prep in advance. Any flatbread can be used. I use packaged naan, which is traditionally Indian, that I often happen to have in my freezer. Pita breads or precooked pizza crusts work wonderfully, as well, and don't require the time to roll out the dough.

SERVES 4

2 cups cooked white beans, drained and rinsed

4 tablespoons extra virgin olive oil

1 teaspoon lemon zest

2 tablespoons fresh lemon juice

2 garlic cloves

Freshly ground pepper and sea salt

4 pieces naan or pita bread

olive oil, for drizzling

2 cups fresh baby spinach

1 cup crumbled feta cheese

¼ cup fresh mint leaves

Pinch of chile flakes

For the white bean purée, combine the beans, olive oil, lemon zest and juice, garlic, and a few generous pinches of salt and pepper in a food processor, and blend until smooth. Be sure to check seasoning to taste. Cover and chill until ready to use.

For the flatbreads, preheat your oven to 400°F or use a preheated grill.

Brush the breads with olive oil and bake for 5 minutes, or until they are toasted and lightly browned. You can also toast them on the grill.

Divide and spread ½ cup of white bean purée onto each flatbread, top with spinach leaves, some crumbled feta cheese, chopped mint leaves, and chile flakes. Sprinkle lightly with salt and pepper. Drizzle again with some olive oil and pop into the hot oven just for a few minutes to wilt the spinach and slightly warm the cheese, or warm on the grill.

Cut and serve warm.

PROSCIUTTO-ASPARAGUS BUNDLES

Nothing says spring like the sweet taste of asparagus, a true marker of the season's triumphant arrival. Bursting with flavor, these bundles can be made in advance, and served as is or warmed up under the broiler for several minutes until the prosciutto is browned and edges are crisp.

—————— **MAKES 2 DOZEN** ——————

24 asparagus spears, trimmed

12 slices prosciutto, cut in half

½ cup extra virgin olive oil

Freshly ground pepper
and sea salt

Preheat the oven to 400°F.

Lay the cut slices of prosciutto on a board.

Gather a bundle of two or three asparagus (you can also use just a single spear) and wrap in the prosciutto. Place onto an oiled baking sheet. Brush with the olive oil and sprinkle with salt and pepper. Roast in the oven for 6–8 minutes or grill briefly, so the asparagus is cooked al dente and just tender.

Serve warm or at room temperature.

chef's note
To serve, let your creativity go wild. After roasting, brush very lightly with a Dijon mustard vinaigrette or freshly grated pecorino cheese, or drizzle with thick and syrupy aged balsamic vinegar.

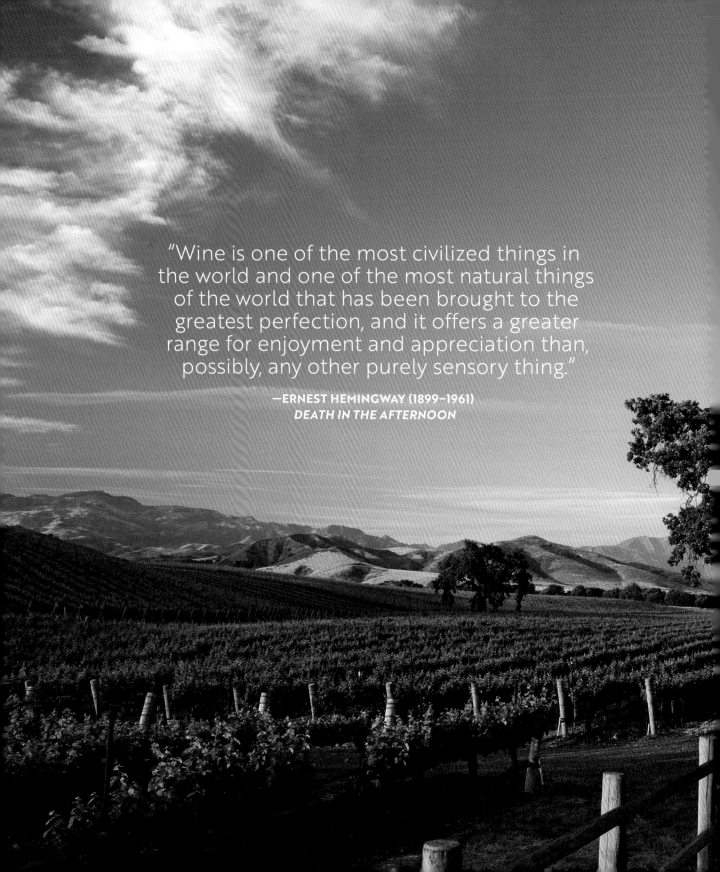

"Wine is one of the most civilized things in the world and one of the most natural things of the world that has been brought to the greatest perfection, and it offers a greater range for enjoyment and appreciation than, possibly, any other purely sensory thing."

—ERNEST HEMINGWAY (1899–1961)
DEATH IN THE AFTERNOON

a taste of cheese

The Ultimate Cheese Board

Parmesan Cheese Straws

Frico Crisps

Cheese-Stuffed Olives

Marinated Pecorino Cheese

Lavender Marcona Almonds

Wine Country Biscuits

Strawberry-Black Pepper Jam

Homemade Mustard

Roasted Tomato Pie

Roasted Squash Tart

Homemade Ricotta

Baked Brie with Caramelized
Apples and Onions

Oven-Baked Brie Fondue

Tomato Panini with Calabrian
Chile Pesto

Bacon Tartine

THE ULTIMATE CHEESE BOARD

A great cheese board enhances any gathering. There's really no wrong way to put one together. There's so much creative freedom with a cheese board that a few guiding principles are all you really need to get started.

Have fun with the display! At the end of the day, you want happy guests, sipping delicious wines, with cheese being the main attraction.

Choose a board big enough to display all the cheeses. A large wooden board, a flat ceramic platter, or even marble or terra cotta floor tiles will do.

Have on hand cheese knives, varying in size and shape for the different cheeses, and remember to have some individual plates and cocktail napkins on the side. (Please don't use mirrors or that big cutting board you cut your holiday meats on!)

Choose three or four different types of cheeses—five, if you've got a crowd.

Go for different places of origin and textures: a soft, bloomy rind from France; a semi-hard Dutch cheese; a harder, aged one from Italy; a blue from England; and, of course, an artisanal cheese from California. Choose cheese made from different milks: goat, sheep and cow's milk cheese; don't forget about blends. Personally, I love a good strong Stilton or creamy Gorgonzola. However, keep in mind that blue cheese is not for everyone, so keep it somewhat isolated, preferably not touching too many other things. It tends to spread its love to its neighbors. Nestling a little dish of honey or jam next to it helps create some boundaries.

When serving cheese as an hors d'oeuvre, plan on 2–3 ounces of each cheese per person. If you're serving the cheese as an after-dinner cheese course, figure one ounce of each cheese per person. When the event is longer, plan for extra. Room-temperature cheeses reveal their flavor subtleties better than cold ones. Be sure to set the cheeses on the counter one hour before you plan on eating, and cut them before you put them on your serving board. That's right. No more sticking a knife in a huge wedge and calling it a day, and, unless your guests are under 10 years old, no cheese "cubes" allowed. Go for strips or wedges (not too thin), or large crumbles that can be eaten in one or two

bites. To keep things tidy and looking presentable, slice your cheeses on a separate board in advance. Keep them covered so they don't dry out, and then arrange them on your serving board. Softer and/or crumbly cheeses, like chèvre and blue, are excellent rolled in chopped nuts or fresh herbs and set in a small bowl, or made into a savory cheese spread. Don't feel you have to put all the bread or crackers out straight away. Keep some ready, tucked away in the kitchen, and it's a quick refill onto the board when they start to get low. Another option is to serve the crackers and breads in separate containers.

For accompaniments, try to include sweet, salty, and briny (pickle-y) choices, and some different nuts for crunch: one bread and cracker, one in-season fruit, one jam, chutney or compote, and one or two savory options, like pickles, olives, salami, mustard, or nuts, to accompany the cheese. Some recipes for these pairings follow. Scatter with a few berries, fresh figs, or a small cluster of grapes. A colorful assortment of many different shapes and textures will make your cheese board pop.

PARMESAN CHEESE STRAWS

Beat 1 egg with 1 tablespoon water. On a floured surface, roll out a thawed frozen puff pastry sheet into a 12-inch square. Brush the dough with the beaten egg and sprinkle with grated Parmesan, sea salt, and a dusting of smoked paprika; you can add a pinch of cayenne pepper if you like a little heat. Cut into 2 dozen strips ½-inch thick; twist each strip. Bake at 375°F for 25 minutes, until golden brown.

FRICO CRISPS

Arrange tablespoon-size mounds of shredded (not grated) Parmesan cheese one inch apart on a silicone mat or a baking paper-lined baking sheet. Sprinkle generously with freshly ground pepper and chopped herbs (rosemary, sage, and/or thyme). Bake at 450°F for 6 to 8 minutes, until crisp. Cool slightly.

CHEESE-STUFFED OLIVES

Stuff 24 large, pitted green olives with a dab of Roquefort or Gorgonzola cheese. Whisk ¼ cup extra virgin olive oil, 2 tablespoons each olive brine and lemon juice, 1 tablespoon gin, 1 teaspoon thyme, and a pinch of sugar; season with sea salt and freshly ground pepper. Pour over the olives and chill.

MARINATED PECORINO CHEESE

Layer ½-inch cheese chunks with fresh herbs, whole peppercorns, and a few pinches of chile flakes in a clean jar. Pour enough extra virgin olive oil in the jar to completely cover the cheese. Let marinate in the refrigerator for at least 8 hours, or overnight, to build the flavor. The marinated cheese will keep for several weeks in a covered jar in the refrigerator.

LAVENDER MARCONA ALMONDS

You will need 2 teaspoons dried lavender, 4 cups Marcona almonds, extra virgin olive oil, granulated sugar, and sea salt. Finely grind the dried lavender in a spice mill or in a mortar and pestle. Preheat the oven to 350°F. Toast the almonds on a baking sheet, for 15 minutes, stirring once, until golden. Transfer to a large bowl and, while still warm, drizzle lightly with 4 tablespoons olive oil. Sprinkle with ½ cup sugar, 1 tablespoon sea salt, and the 2 teaspoons of ground lavender. Toss to coat. Best served warm. These almonds also make a great edible gift, divided into cellophane bags and tied with twine and a sprig of fresh lavender.

WINE COUNTRY BISCUITS

These ultimate crunchy, satisfying bites are inspired by Italian *taralli*, a street snack common all over the southern half of the Italian peninsula. Similar in texture to breadsticks or pretzels, they can be made sweet or savory. A warning—they are very addictive.

—————————————— **MAKES 2 DOZEN** ——————————————

4 cups all-purpose flour

1 tablespoon sea salt

1 tablespoon chopped fresh rosemary

1 teaspoon freshly ground pepper

1 teaspoon toasted fennel seeds

7 ounces dry white wine

½ cup extra virgin olive oil

Coarse sea salt

Mix the flour, salt, rosemary, pepper, and fennel seeds in a large bowl.

Use your hands to form a hole in the center. Pour in the wine and olive oil.

Mix with a wooden spoon from the center out to form the dough or prepare in a mixer with a dough hook. Pour the dough out onto a lightly floured workspace and knead 4–5 minutes, until it is smooth and elastic. Place the dough in a lightly oiled bowl, cover and allow to rest for at least 30 minutes at room temperature.

Working in quarter portions, roll the dough into cigar thickness, cutting into ½-inch pieces with a knife or pastry cutter. Then roll each piece thinner, to the size of a thick pencil, 5 inches long, and attach the two ends, kneading the ends back and forth together lightly with your fingertips to attach. Repeat until you've finished shaping all the pieces.

Preheat the oven to 400°F.

Bring a large pot of salted water to a boil. Working in batches, drop 6 to 8 pieces into the boiling water and boil until they float to the top. Remove with a slotted spoon onto a kitchen towel and allow to dry.

Once they are dry, transfer to a parchment paper-lined baking sheet, sprinkle lightly with coarse sea salt, and bake for 30–40 minutes, until lightly browned, rotating the pan halfway through.

Allow to cool completely. Store the biscuits in an airtight container at room temperature.

These are good for up to a few weeks.

STRAWBERRY-BLACK PEPPER JAM

This is an excellent jam. If you have never thought of black pepper as an ingredient in strawberry jam, this recipe will change your mind! The black pepper gives it just a little edge, not overpowering at all, and I use an aged balsamic vinegar. The jam goes really well with cheese or as a glaze for meat. For my own use, just a few half-pint jars is enough. The true joy of small-batch canning is that there's no need to pull out a giant pot to sterilize the jars, as I store these in the fridge for immediate consumption. This small-scale recipe is perfect for that, and it's also a great use of leftover strawberries, instead of filling up the freezer with them. I make this preserve as gifts for my clients to share my love.

MAKES 2 CUPS

4 cups fresh ripe sliced strawberries, washed and hulled

½ cup honey or brown sugar

1 split vanilla bean

1 tablespoon fresh lemon juice

½ cup balsamic vinegar

2 teaspoons freshly ground pepper

Pinch of sea salt

In a bowl, stir together the sliced berries, honey, and vanilla bean. Set aside for about an hour to draw out the juices from the berries, before making the jam.

In a large heavy-bottomed skillet (cast iron is perfect) over medium-high heat, add the berry mixture with all the juices, and the lemon juice, and stir often with a wooden spoon to break up any large chunks of berries, about 10 minutes. Add the balsamic vinegar, ground pepper, and a generous pinch of salt, and stir to combine. Simmer an additional 5 minutes to thicken.

Pour into clean glass jars, cover and cool for a few hours, then refrigerate and use within 3 weeks. Serve with cheeses, glazed meats, or as a great option for a breakfast jam.

Follow proper canning and sterilization procedures for shelf-stable storage.

HOMEMADE MUSTARD

If you are a mustard lover like me, making your own homemade version is easier than you would think. There are so many variations: You can make your own spicy, sweet, and/or hot mustard just by adjusting a few of the ingredients to change it up. Using a blender is the easiest method, or use a mortar and pestle. If you'd like to make the process easier, just grind the mustard seeds in advance until you like what you see.

MAKES 3 HALF-PINT JARS

1 cup white wine vinegar or red wine vinegar

1 cup white wine or red wine

¼ cup water

1 tablespoon chopped shallots

1 bay leaf

1 teaspoon peppercorns

3 allspice berries

1 cup yellow mustard seeds (or combine ¾ cup yellow with ¼ cup brown mustard seeds)

¼ cup brown sugar or honey

2 tablespoons dry mustard

2 teaspoons dried tarragon

1 tablespoon sea salt

½ teaspoon freshly ground pepper

In a small saucepan, combine the vinegar, wine, water, shallots, bay leaf, peppercorns, and allspice berries. Bring to a simmer and cook for one minute. Strain the flavored liquid over the mustard seeds. Soak the mustard seeds in the vinegar solution in a glass jar for at least 12, and up to 24 hours.

Place the soaked mustard seeds with all of their liquid in a blender. Add the sugar or honey, dry mustard, tarragon, salt, and pepper. Blend until thickened and the seeds are coarsely ground, 1–2 minutes, or make a grainy mustard by only blending ½ of the seeds, and stirring the rest into the blended mixture afterward. Transfer the mixture to small, sterilized jars and store in your refrigerator for up to 2 months. The mustard can be quite spicy at first and will mellow out after a couple of days.

chef's note
Substituting different wine vinegars and wines (red and white), alternating other herbs in place of tarragon, preparing the mustard in a mortar and pestle (which was my first attempt), or using a different ratio of mustard seeds (some whole and some ground), will expand your collection of mustards.

For a green mustard, blend in ½ cup parsley, or other fresh green herbs.

ROASTED TOMATO PIE

As soon as the first tomatoes hit the market, I collect a basketful for my favorite savory summertime pie with roasted tomatoes, fragrant herbs, and a delicious cheese mixture with a homemade crust. A store-bought crust can be used in a pinch, but taking the extra time to make this cornmeal crust is certainly worth it.

SERVES 6–8

For the crust

1 cup all-purpose flour

¾ cup yellow cornmeal

½ teaspoon sea salt

1 stick cold unsalted butter, cut into ½-inch pieces

3 tablespoons plus 1 cup shredded manchego cheese, divided

Ice water

For the filling

2 pounds mixed tomatoes

Extra virgin olive oil

Freshly ground pepper and sea salt

1 large onion, sliced thin

½ cup ricotta cheese

3 tablespoons fresh snipped chives

3 tablespoons chopped fresh parsley

1 teaspoon chopped fresh thyme

To make the crust, pulse the flour, cornmeal, and salt in a food processor to combine. Add the butter and 3 tablespoons manchego. Pulse until the mixture looks like coarse meal. Drizzle in 4 tablespoons ice water and pulse until the dough just comes together. Add more ice water by the tablespoon, as needed. Turn out the dough onto a sheet of plastic wrap and pat into a flat disk. Wrap and refrigerate for 1 hour, until firm.

Meanwhile, preheat the oven to 375°F. Slice the tomatoes, lay them out in a single layer on a baking pan, sprinkle with 1 teaspoon salt and 2 tablespoons olive oil, and roast for 30 minutes.

After chilling, roll the dough into a 12-inch round and transfer to a 10-inch pie plate or tart pan. Fold the dough overhang under itself and crimp the edges. Pierce the bottom of the crust all over with a fork.

Line the crust with foil, then fill with dried beans to weigh it down. Bake at 375°F for 20 minutes. Remove the foil and beans and continue baking 10–15 minutes more, until golden brown all over. Transfer to a rack to cool.

Over medium heat, sauté the onion in 1 tablespoon olive oil for 15 minutes, until lightly caramelized. Set aside to cool. Combine the remaining 1 cup manchego, the ricotta cheese, 2 tablespoons each of chives and parsley, thyme, ½ teaspoon salt and a few grinds of pepper, and cooled sautéed onions. Spread this mixture in the baked crust and arrange the tomatoes on top. Drizzle with a tablespoon of olive oil and a few grinds of pepper. Bake at 375°F for 15 minutes, just to warm the cheese through.

Serve warm, scattered with the remaining fresh herbs.

ROASTED SQUASH TART

Whenever I make this tart, it reminds me of Holland. Not that this dish is particularly Dutch, but the use of Gouda cheese somehow brings back memories of my travels around the Netherlands. Gouda, or "How-da" as the locals say, is a cheese named after the city of Gouda. Did you know it is one of the most popular cheeses in the world? It accounts for 60 percent of the world's cheese consumption. Who knew? Aged Gouda, like Old Amsterdam, with its brittle, crumbly, crystalline texture and complex burnt-caramel flavor, is an excellent choice to use for this recipe. There are many types of Gouda. You can use your favorite. Goat's milk Gouda and smoked Gouda are also good options here.

SERVES 4

4 cups mushrooms, cremini, chanterelle, oyster, sliced

2 large leeks, white to light green parts (see chef's note)

3 cups butternut squash, peeled, cut into ½-inch cubes

Extra virgin olive oil

Freshly ground pepper and sea salt

1 sheet of puff pastry, thawed

1 teaspoon fresh thyme leaves

Pinch of chile flakes

1 cup grated aged Gouda cheese

Fresh chopped herbs (parsley and chives), for garnish

Heat the oven to 400°F. On a large parchment paper-lined baking sheet, toss the mushrooms and leeks with 2 tablespoons olive oil, salt, and pepper and spread out evenly. On another large parchment paper-lined baking sheet, toss the squash with 2 tablespoon olive oil, salt, and pepper and spread out evenly, as well. Roast both pans of vegetables for about 25 minutes, until lightly browned at the edges. Don't let the vegetables get too brown or overcooked, as they will be cooked again. Set aside to cool. To prep ahead, you can roast the vegetables earlier in the day.

Lightly oil a large baking sheet. Roll the puff pastry into a rectangle to thin out the dough to ¼ inch, then transfer to the oiled baking sheet. (It does not have to be perfectly shaped.)

Spread the mushroom-leek mixture onto the dough, sprinkle with fresh thyme and chile flakes, and top with the grated cheese, followed by the roasted squash. Sprinkle lightly with salt and drizzle with some olive oil. In a 400°F oven, bake 25–30 minutes, until golden brown all over.

Serve warm, with more fresh chopped herbs.

chef's note

Leeks are often full of sand and dirt because the soil is pushed up high around them as they are grown. Here is an easy tip for getting your leeks clean: Slice the fibrous dark green portion off and save for broths and soups. Cut the bottom portion in half lengthwise, then slice thin and plunge into a bowl of warm water to remove all the silt. Drain and rinse well once more, shaking the water off in a colander. The leeks are now ready to cook.

HOMEMADE RICOTTA

If you've never made homemade cheese before, ricotta is one of the easiest to tackle first. Not only is it a fun DIY project, it tastes perfect on just about everything. The milk and cream you use may affect the characteristics of your cheese, so preparing it with organic milk and cream is ideal. Distilled vinegar gives a clean flavor, and soft, tender curds. Lemon juice, also recommended, works very well—it gives the ricotta a slight citrus tang. After draining, the ricotta can be served fresh, drizzled with local honey or with sliced fruits or roasted grapes. It's wonderful baked or sprinkled with chopped garlic, herbs or chopped greens. I like it on top of toast in the morning, or on freshly picked baby lettuces simply dressed with extra virgin olive oil and sea salt, and garnished with fresh lemon zest or pesto.

MAKES 2 CUPS

---

2 quarts whole milk

1 cup heavy cream

½ teaspoon sea salt

3 tablespoons distilled white vinegar or fresh lemon juice

Line a colander with four layers of cheesecloth or two layers of food-safe paper towels, and set over a large bowl.

Slowly bring the milk, cream, and salt to a boil in a 6-quart heavy pot over moderate heat, stirring occasionally to prevent scorching and being careful to not let it boil over. (The milk should register 165°F on an instant-read thermometer.)

Add the vinegar or lemon juice, then reduce the heat to low and simmer, stirring gently and constantly, 2–4 minutes, until the mixture curdles.

Using a slotted spoon or wire skimmer, transfer all the curds to the cloth-lined colander, wrap and cover the exposed top with the sides of the cheesecloth, and allow to drain until desired texture is reached. Store in a covered container in the refrigerator for up to 5 days.

Drainage Times
Under 5 minutes—moist and creamy consistency with small, tender curds.

20–30 minutes—moist and spreadable, not runny; small, tender curds with a cottage cheese-like consistency. Best used for savory applications like lasagna or ravioli fillings or spreads.

At least 2 hours, or up to overnight in the refrigerator—firm, dry, crumbly curds that can be easily molded into firm shapes. Best used for pastry, such as ricotta pancakes or tortas.

BAKED BRIE WITH CARAMELIZED APPLES AND ONIONS

Although this is often served *en croute*, wrapped in puff pastry, I have skipped the extra calories of the buttery pastry in this version and topped the melting cheese with the tender, sweet, caramelized apple-and-onion mixture instead. The only trick to this recipe is in the cooking of the onions. I like onions that are deeply caramelized, not just sautéed. That requires a bit of time in the kitchen, stirring the onions so they don't burn. The satisfying thing is that the onions can be made up to 2 days in advance and stored in the refrigerator until you are ready to use them.

SERVES 4–6

2 tablespoons unsalted butter

2 tablespoons extra virgin olive oil

3 cups sliced onions (3 large onions)

4 garlic cloves, minced

1 cup apples, peeled, cored, and sliced thin

1½ teaspoons sea salt

Freshly ground pepper

½ cup dry white wine

1 (2-pound) French Brie round

Crackers, baguette slices, and crostini, to serve

Heat a very large heavy skillet (cast iron works best) over medium-high heat.

Add the butter, olive oil, and onions and sauté 15 minutes, until tender and well caramelized.

Add the garlic and apple slices and cook for another 2 minutes to soften the apples. Add salt and pepper and stir to scrape any brown bits on the bottom. Stir in the wine and continue to cook until the liquid evaporates, then cool. (The onion mixture can also be prepared up to 2 days ahead and stored in an airtight container in the refrigerator.)

Preheat the oven to 350°F. Unwrap the Brie and cut off only the top rind of the cheese, leaving sides and bottom intact. Place the Brie, cut side up, in a round ceramic baking dish slightly larger than the Brie round. (A 9-inch deep dish pie plate or ceramic quiche pan works well, too.) Top the Brie evenly with the caramelized onion mixture. Place the dish on a baking pan to catch any cheese drips. Bake 30 minutes, until melted, oozing and bubbling. Remove from the oven and transfer to a heatproof platter.

Serve with crackers, baguette slices, and crostini.

OVEN-BAKED BRIE FONDUE

This fondue is reminiscent of the traditional dish served in the proper Swiss way, which comes with cubes of bread and white wine, kirsch, or a tisane or herbal tea to drink. According to Swiss lore, any other drink—be it water, juice, or beer—will "cause the melted cheese to form a giant ball in your stomach, leaving you with debilitating indigestion." Yes, it sounds silly, but do you really want to risk it? This is a shortcut take on Swiss fondue, but much easier to prepare, especially if you don't own a fondue pot.

SERVES 4

1 round of Brie, 9 ounces or larger (or similar cheese in a small wooden box)

2 garlic cloves, chopped fine

2 teaspoons extra virgin olive oil

Few sprigs of thyme

For serving

Crudités of cauliflower, carrots, radishes, or other seasonal vegetables

Slices of toasted or grilled bread

Preheat the oven to 375°F. Unwrap the cheese and cut off the top rind.

Put the cheese back into the wooden box and set on a baking pan.

If your cheese doesn't come in a box, you can set it in an ovenproof ceramic baking dish, more or less the same size as the cheese.

Scatter the chopped garlic over the cheese. Pour the olive oil on the cheese and add a few sprigs of thyme. Bake the cheese for 15 minutes or until it's warm, melting, and somewhat runny.

Serve with the crudités and bread for dipping, shots of Kirschwasser, and a pot of herbal tea.

TOMATO PANINI WITH CALABRIAN CHILE PESTO

This is really a suggestion rather than a recipe because you can go wild with the variety of panini you can create in your own home. I used a crusty ciabatta loaf and experimented with both roasted and freshly sliced tomatoes. I tried different cheeses, too. A smoky mozzarella, fresh mozzarella, and the creaminess of ricotta made for an ooey-gooey messy grilled cheese sandwich—the very best kind.

MAKES 2 SANDWICHES

4 slices of your favorite bread

½ cup Calabrian chile pesto (see recipe below)

Fresh sliced, or roasted tomatoes

Freshly ground pepper and sea salt

1 ball fresh mozzarella

2 slices smoked mozzarella

½ cup ricotta cheese (see recipe, page 65)

Preheat the oven to broil or use a panini press.

Make the Calabrian chile pesto and spread the mixture onto two slices of bread. Top with the fresh sliced or roasted tomatoes and cheese. If broiling the sandwiches, place them open-faced on a baking pan and broil until the cheese is melted, then top with the second slice of bread. If using a panini press, grill the sandwiches until the bread is browned and the cheese is melted.

Slice and serve warm.

CALABRIAN CHILE PESTO

1 cup walnuts

½ cup sun-dried tomatoes

6 Calabrian chile peppers in oil

2 garlic cloves

½ cup Parmesan, grated

½ cup fresh parsley leaves

⅓ cup extra virgin olive oil

1 teaspoon sea salt and freshly ground pepper

In a food processor, pulse the walnuts and dried tomatoes until crumbly. Add the chiles, garlic, Parmesan, and parsley with the olive oil, salt, and a few grinds of pepper. Blend to combine the pesto. This can keep for a week or so in a covered container in the refrigerator.

chef's note
Calabrian chiles—small, round, and spicy peppers from Calabria, Italy—are dark red in color and are aged on the vine to ensure a more potent heat and fruitier taste. They typically are pickled or stuffed and packed in olive oil, and are excellent on pizza and in pesto. If you can't find Calabrian chiles, the pesto can be made with your favorite pickled pepper just as easily. Adding this pesto will jazz up your pasta dishes, stews, soups, and salsa.

BACON TARTINE

What makes a classic, crispy grilled cheese sandwich even better? Why, *bacon* of course! This open-faced tartine with bacon and spinach on thick artisan bread slathered with Dijon mustard is miles above your typical American cheese-and-white-bread variety.

--- **SERVES 4** ---

2 teaspoons extra virgin olive oil

6 ounces fresh spinach or chard, washed

¼ teaspoon sea salt

Freshly ground pepper

4 slices thick-cut bacon, cut crosswise into ¼-inch pieces

4 large bread slices from a rustic, day-old loaf, ½-inch thick

Dijon mustard

4 ounces raclette or Gruyère cheese

Heat the olive oil in a medium skillet over medium heat. Add the spinach, season with salt and a few grinds of pepper, and cook, stirring for one minute until just wilted. Drain, cool, and squeeze out excess water.

In a separate pan, fry the bacon pieces over medium heat for 3–4 minutes, until just crisped. Remove and drain on paper towels.

Put the bread slices on a baking pan and toast lightly on both sides under a broiler (or use a toaster and place toasted slices on a baking pan).

Brush the toast lightly with the mustard. Divide and spread the greens among the four toasts, sprinkle with the crisp bacon, and top each toast with slices of cheese.

Broil for 2–3 minutes, not too close to the heat, until browned and melted, or bake the tartines in your countertop toaster oven.

Serve hot, melted, and gooey, with some pickles on the side.

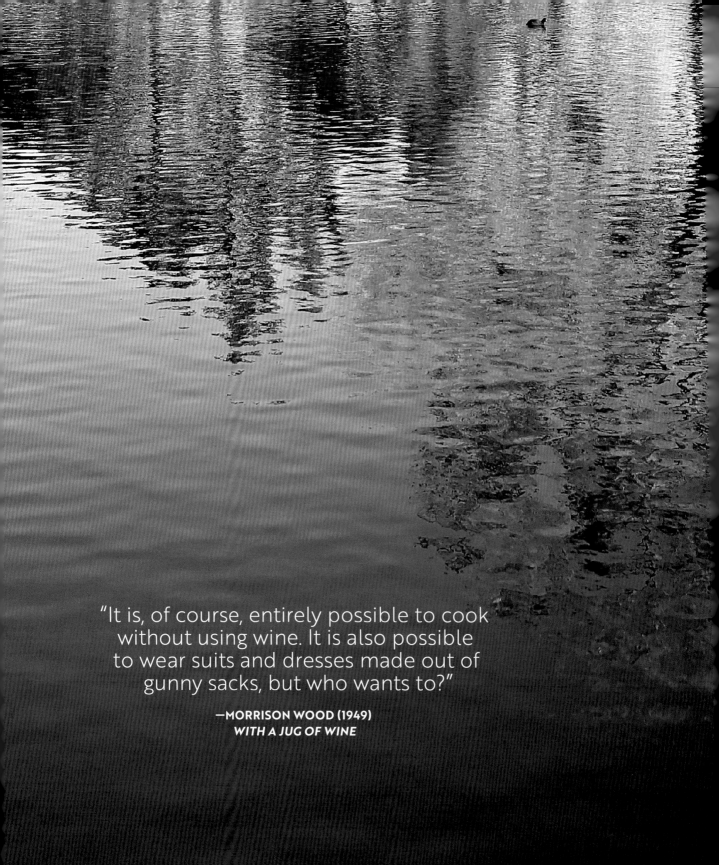

"It is, of course, entirely possible to cook without using wine. It is also possible to wear suits and dresses made out of gunny sacks, but who wants to?"

—MORRISON WOOD (1949)
WITH A JUG OF WINE

with white wine

Roasted Tomato and Fennel Soup

Chilled Cucumber Soup

Roasted Corn and Crab Chowder

Crispy Prosciutto and Melon

Fish Parcels with Arugula-Walnut Pesto

Griddled Salmon Cakes

Cucumber-Grapefruit Crab Salad

Grilled Scallops

Pan-Roasted Fish with Garlic, Lentils, and Chiles

Good Friday Fish with Crispy Dill

Parmesan-Crusted Chicken

ROASTED TOMATO AND FENNEL SOUP

I grow a few varieties of tomatoes in my raised vegetable garden at home, and when my plants start getting taller than me, I start picking the ideal mature fruit to start ripening. When bowls of ripe juicy tomatoes overflow on my kitchen counter, I toss them with some great-tasting olive oil to be roasted. Experience the real essence of tomatoes, served either hot or chilled, in this delicious soup, plated with your favorite grilled cheese sandwich. Make a double batch and freeze extra for a rainy day.

SERVES 6

3 pounds ripe tomatoes,
  cut in half lengthwise

Extra virgin olive oil

2 garlic cloves, sliced thin

1 medium onion, sliced thin

1 fennel bulb, sliced thin

1 quart vegetable stock or water

½ cup white wine

½ teaspoon crushed
  fennel seeds

¼ teaspoon chile flakes

2 tablespoons balsamic vinegar

Freshly ground pepper
  and sea salt

Preheat the oven to 400°F. Toss together the tomatoes, ¼ cup olive oil, and 1 teaspoon salt. Spread the tomatoes in one layer on a baking sheet and roast for 45 minutes, until tomatoes are blistered but not dried.

In a heavy-bottomed 4-quart pot over medium heat, sauté the garlic, onion, and fennel with ½ teaspoon salt and a few grinds of pepper in 3 tablespoons olive oil for 8–10 minutes, until the onions and fennel are soft and fragrant.

Add the oven-roasted tomatoes, including the liquid on the baking sheet, the vegetable stock or water, wine, crushed fennel, and chile flakes. Simmer, covered, for 20 minutes. Using a handheld immersion blender directly in the pot, or a Vitamix, purée the soup until it is smooth. Taste and adjust the seasoning with more salt, as needed, and a few grinds of pepper; then stir in the balsamic vinegar to finish.

chef's note
Using a mortar and pestle to finely crush the fennel seeds is an easy way to grind the seeds; freshly grinding whole spices releases the oils for a very fresh taste.

CHILLED CUCUMBER SOUP

Serve a cold and refreshing soup to beat the sizzling summer temperatures and "stay as cool as a cucumber." This soup gets its creaminess from Greek yogurt, only takes minutes to make, and is a welcome simple summer starter. A great way to use the cucumbers from your vegetable patch, it is ideal for a garden party at home, or keep the soup chilled in a thermos to take to the beach or a picnic.

SERVES 4

4 cups cucumbers, peeled, seeded, and sliced

1 ½ cups plain Greek yogurt

¼ cup dry white wine

1 green onion, chopped coarse

1 garlic clove, sliced

1 tablespoon snipped fresh dill

2 tablespoons fresh tarragon leaves

¼ cup flat-leaf parsley leaves

¼ cup extra virgin olive oil, plus more to drizzle

Additional chopped green onion and snipped fresh dill

Lemon

Freshly ground pepper and sea salt

In a colander set over a bowl, toss the sliced cucumbers with 1 teaspoon salt and let stand for 30 minutes, then gently pat dry with a paper towel. Place the salted cucumbers, yogurt, white wine, green onion, garlic, fresh herbs, and olive oil in a Vitamix or regular blender. Cover and blend until smooth; taste and adjust seasoning with more salt, as needed, and a few grinds of pepper, then chill until ready to serve. Ladle the soup into bowls, drizzle with olive oil, and garnish with additional green onion, dill, and a squeeze of fresh lemon juice.

chef's note
if you are using young Persian or English cucumbers, it may not be necessary to remove the seeds, as they are tender and sweet. Make the serving more substantial by topping bowls of this soup with slices of ripe avocado, poached shrimp, and rustic garlic croutons.

ROASTED CORN AND CRAB CHOWDER

In summer, my mind drifts back to the weathered crab shacks of the Eastern Shore where you look out over the Chesapeake Bay with your feet in the sand, waiting for your name to be called for dinner. Born and raised in the state of Maryland, I know a thing or two about local East Coast seafood. Start this recipe by roasting the corn on the cob, or use leftover roasted or grilled corn. This chowder, swimming with chunks of sweet lump crab meat, comes alive with roasted chiles and a splash of fresh lime juice.

SERVES 6

2 tablespoons unsalted butter

2 tablespoons extra virgin olive oil

2 medium onions, diced small (2 cups)

½ cup celery, diced small

½ cup fennel bulb, diced small

6 ears of fresh white corn, roasted on the cob

2 garlic cloves, chopped fine

½ cup white wine

2 medium Yukon gold potatoes, peeled, cut into 1-inch chunks

1 quart chicken or vegetable broth

1 teaspoon ground cumin

1 teaspoon ground coriander

4 roasted poblano green chiles, peeled and chopped (to yield 1 cup)

2 cups fresh lump crab meat

Freshly ground pepper and sea salt

½ cup fresh cilantro, chopped

2 limes, for juice

In a 4-quart heavy-bottomed pot on medium-high heat, melt the butter with the olive oil and sauté the onions, celery, and fennel with 1 teaspoon of salt, for 8–10 minutes. Lower the heat, if needed, and sauté until the onions are softened and starting to brown. While those are cooking, cut the kernels of corn away from the cobs. Once the onions, celery, and fennel have browned, add the garlic and white wine and cook for a minute more. Add the diced potatoes and broth to the pot with a pinch of salt, followed by the cumin and coriander.

Maintain a simmer and cook for 10–15 minutes, until the potatoes are just cooked through.

Add the corn to the pot and cook for 5 minutes, then add the chopped roasted poblanos.

If you like a creamy, thick base for your chowder without adding cream, you can use a handheld immersion blender, or a Vitamix or regular blender, to purée one-third of the soup at this point. After blending, taste and adjust seasoning with more salt, as needed, and a few grinds of pepper. Add the fresh crab meat and chopped cilantro, gently stir to combine, and finish with a squeeze of fresh lime juice just before serving.

chef's note
Green chiles are always better if you roast them first, blackening them either over a grill, on a gas stove, or under a broiler, to remove the tough outer skin. After charring, place the peppers in a bowl, cover and allow them to steam for 15 minutes before scraping off the blackened skin and removing the seeds.

CRISPY PROSCIUTTO AND MELON

Prosciutto and melon make a simple, elegant summer appetizer. If you can, try using the famed Prosciutto di Parma or search out Spain's Jamón Serrano. These sweet, salty, and juicy nibbles are perfect served with a chilled glass of Prosecco, Italy's most widely known sparkling white wine—it doesn't play second fiddle to Champagne any longer.

SERVES 4

- 1 small Crenshaw or other orange-fleshed melon
- ¼ pound thinly sliced Prosciutto di Parma or Jamón Serrano, cut in half lengthwise
- 1 small bunch basil, leaves chopped thin
- Freshly ground pepper and sea salt
- Extra virgin olive oil and balsamic vinegar

Prepare the melon by first cutting it in half lengthwise and scooping out the seeds. Then, scoop out mini melon balls or simply slice away the peel and cut into small cubes. Be aware that the melon closest to the rind doesn't have much flavor. Chill the melon until ready to serve.

Preheat the oven to 375°F. Lay each half slice of prosciutto inside a mini muffin tin. Overlap the sides to make a "cup" and bake for 12 minutes, or so. Remove from the oven and allow to cool for a couple minutes. Place the prosciutto on a paper towel to drain off any excess fat. The prosciutto "cups" will firm up once cooled.

In a small bowl, combine the melon and fresh basil with a dash of olive oil, ¼ teaspoon salt, and a few grinds of pepper, and spoon into each cup.

Drizzle with a few drops of balsamic vinegar just before serving.

chef's note
I have prepared this recipe with many other herbs, depending on the season; try it with fresh mint, mild tarragon, even cilantro. Add some fresh mozzarella, and you can't go wrong with this tasty *aperitivo*.

FISH PARCELS WITH ARUGULA-WALNUT PESTO

There are countless recipes for pesto, and just about every one includes nuts. This healthy, peppery, bright sauce has a little bit of a kick to it, and comes together in minutes. It is made with a few simple ingredients, including walnuts which contain omega-3 fatty acids (a natural food element that reduces inflammation). Freshly toasted nuts taste so much better; you basically warm them in a skillet on the stove until the edges are golden and you begin to notice the roasted fragrance. The beauty of this particular pesto is that it keeps its gorgeous green color for days, even after you warm it up. It is the perfect sauce to pair with fish, perk up pasta or gnocchi, or be used as a great spread on grilled chicken sandwiches. Have fun searching for fun ways to add it to your weekly cooking!

SERVES 4

For the pesto

2 cups arugula, washed and dried

1 cup fresh basil leaves

½ cup walnuts, toasted

4 garlic cloves

2 lemons, zest and juice

Pinch of chile flakes

Extra virgin olive oil

For the fish parcels

4 (6 to 8-ounce) portions of mild white fish

Freshly ground pepper and sea salt

For the pesto
Blend the following ingredients in a food processor or combine in a mortar and pestle: arugula, basil leaves, walnuts, using only 2 garlic cloves, 2 teaspoons lemon zest, a pinch of chile flakes, and ½ cup olive oil with 1 teaspoon salt. Set aside to top the fish parcels and be sure to use any leftover pesto within 1 week.

For the fish parcels
For the four portions, cut four sheets of baking paper large enough to enclose a fish fillet, and four sheets of aluminum foil 1–2 inches larger than the baking paper. Lay the four sheets of foil out on your counter and place a sheet of baking paper on top of a sheet of foil, drizzling each paper with ½ teaspoon olive oil.

Set the portions of fish on the baking paper, sprinkle each one with salt and a few grinds of pepper, and top with a few garlic slices and a bit of lemon zest. Squeeze the lemon juice over the fish, and drizzle each portion with ½ teaspoon olive oil.

Bring the sides of the foil and baking paper to meet in the center and fold or scrunch together to seal. Place the parcels in an ovenproof dish and bake for 20 minutes, until the fish is cooked through. To serve, either remove the fish from their wrapping onto a plate and serve with the pesto on the side, or simply put the paper-wrapped parcels on plates, open them up, spoon on the pesto, and serve immediately.

GRIDDLED SALMON CAKES

My Grandma Hilda, who was the "Chef" in our family, frequently made these salmon cakes in the style of Maryland crab cakes. They are mostly salmon with very little filler, which makes them always disappear fast. These cakes were well loved by all the kids in our family. They don't even need sauce—a generous squeeze of lemon does the trick for these fantastic little fish cakes.

SERVES 6

1 large egg

2 tablespoons good-quality mayonnaise

1 teaspoon Worcestershire sauce

2 teaspoons Old Bay Seasoning

1 teaspoon dry mustard

¼ teaspoon sea salt

¼ teaspoon freshly ground pepper

¼ cup red onion, peeled, diced fine

2 garlic cloves, minced

2 tablespoons fresh parsley, chopped fine

1 pound cooked salmon, chilled

1 cup panko bread crumbs

Vegetable oil or extra virgin olive oil, for cooking

2 teaspoons butter, for cooking

Few lemons, cut into wedges

In a large mixing bowl, start by beating the egg with the mayonnaise and Worcestershire sauce. Add the Old Bay Seasoning, mustard, salt, pepper, chopped onion, garlic, and parsley. Flake the cooked salmon with a fork, remove any bones, and add to the ingredients in the bowl along with 2 tablespoons of bread crumbs, gently folding the mixture together until just combined. Shape into 12 small patties (or 6 medium). I find it's easiest to portion the cakes using an ice cream scoop and then forming them into 1-inch thick patties. Place the remaining bread crumbs onto a shallow dish and roll the cakes to coat the outside of each portion. Cover and refrigerate for at least 1 hour.

Heat 1 tablespoon oil and 1 teaspoon butter in a large pan over medium heat, and once the butter is done sizzling, add half of the salmon cakes and sauté 3–4 minutes per side, or until golden brown. If the cakes start to brown too quickly, reduce the heat. Remove onto a paper towel-lined plate. Add 1 tablespoon oil and 1 teaspoon butter, and repeat with the remaining salmon cakes.

Serve warm with fresh lemon.

chef's note
Freshly cooked salmon is best, but leftover cooked or canned salmon can be substituted. If the mixture is too moist to hold the shape, add more bread crumbs; if it's too dry, add an extra tablespoon of mayo.

CUCUMBER-GRAPEFRUIT CRAB SALAD

This salad is wonderful for your next annual "ladies who lunch" affair, or really for any occasion. It needs very little dressing, allowing the subtle flavor of the fresh crab to shine through. The tart-sweet ruby red grapefruit segments pair well with a dry sparkling wine with high acidity. Substitute fresh tangerines for the grapefruit when in season.

SERVES 4

1 large pink grapefruit (or 2 clementine tangerines), skinned and segmented, all pith and seeds removed

2 tablespoons grapeseed oil

2 teaspoons white wine vinegar

2 teaspoons whole grain mustard

1 lime, zested and juiced

1 teaspoon honey

8 ounces fresh crab meat

¼ cup green onion, chopped fine

1 tablespoon chives, snipped

Freshly ground pepper and sea salt

1 leaf lettuce, washed and dried

1 small cucumber, peeled and sliced thin

Peel and segment the grapefruit or tangerines over a bowl to catch the juice. Reserve the juice and grapefruit pieces separately. In a small bowl, combine the oil, vinegar, mustard, lime zest and juice, honey, ¼ teaspoon salt and the reserved grapefruit juice, and whisk together for the dressing.

In another bowl, combine the crab meat, green onion, and chives. Add 2 tablespoons dressing and toss to combine. Taste and adjust the seasoning with more salt and a few grinds of freshly ground pepper.

Compose the lettuce leaves on individual chilled plates or a serving platter. Add a spoonful of crab meat salad and surround with the grapefruit segments and the cucumber slices. Drizzle each plate with more dressing on the lettuces.

GRILLED SCALLOPS

Scallops are a true seafood treasure; nothing compares with the plump texture and subtle flavor—I just love them! Grilled in the shell—I bought my shells online from Florida—they are ideal for an elegant first course or a romantic candle-lit dinner. It's a classic, distinctive dish and surprisingly easy to cook. If you'd like something crisp, refreshing, and acidic to cleanse the palate and to match the seafood's richness, you can go for a Chardonnay or, for a contrast, choose a Sauvignon Blanc.

SERVES 6

---

12 large diver sea scallops, cleaned and dried

Freshly ground pepper and sea salt

8 tablespoons salted butter

2 tablespoons extra virgin olive oil

4 garlic cloves, minced

Juice of 1 large lemon

Pinch of chile flakes

Splash of white wine

Large handful of fresh parsley

Lime wedges

Preheat a wood or gas grill, then sprinkle the scallops with freshly ground pepper and sea salt.

Make the garlic butter in a small saucepan, which you can do right on the grill or over medium heat. Melt the butter and oil, swirl around the pan to speed the melting, and once the fat begins to smoke, carefully add the garlic, lemon juice, chile flakes, and a pinch of salt and pepper. The longer those flavors hang out the better. Give the mixture a good stir, then set aside.

Place 2 scallops inside each shell set on a large pan. Splash each shell with a small amount of wine. Using tongs, place each shell directly on the preheated grill, carefully positioning the shells so they can't tip over. Lower the lid of the grill and cook for 4 to 6 minutes, or until cooked through, turning the scallops in the shell halfway with tongs. Carefully remove the shells to a serving platter and drizzle 1 tablespoon of the melted garlic-chile butter over each one. Roughly chop and scatter the parsley leaves over the scallops and serve right away with the lime wedges for garnish.

chef's note
This starter is equally delicious made with shrimp, or with both shrimp and scallops—an outstanding combo. For the combined version, use half a pound of large raw shrimp, peeled and deveined, with tails off, along with the scallops, and cook over the grill as described above.

Have some extra lemon or lime wedges on hand when serving, if anyone wants an extra squeeze of juice.

PAN-ROASTED FISH WITH GARLIC, LENTILS, AND CHILES

Pan roasting is one of the easiest, most delicious ways to cook fish. While living in Spain, I bought fish straight off the boat from the local fishermen. Roasting the fish in its skin keeps the meat juicier than using skinless fillets, and the skin gets beautifully crisp, contrasting with the tenderness of the meat. A good-quality, fresh fish needs little to taste good; a little sea salt and pepper, some fresh herbs, and a squeeze of lemon juice. Plated with Le Puy lentils, the fish makes an impressive and gorgeous main dish.

SERVES 4

2 (3 to 4-pound) whole branzino, gutted, scaled, and filleted (this is a Mediterranean sea bass, a mild white fish)

Extra virgin olive oil

Freshly ground pepper and sea salt

2 lemons, sliced

4 garlic cloves, sliced

4 tablespoons salted butter

Several sprigs of fresh flat-leaf parsley

Lentils (see chef's note)

Preheat a heavy cast iron skillet on medium heat.

Use a sharp knife to make three diagonal slices, ½-inch deep, on the skin side of each fish fillet. Generously sprinkle both sides of the fish with salt and pepper.

Pan roast the fillets in 2 teaspoons olive oil for 4–5 minutes, skin side down, to crisp up the skin. Gently flip the fillet over for a few minutes more, until the flesh is opaque.

When the fish is cooked, remove to a serving platter, place skin side up on top of the lentils, and arrange a lemon slice into the three slits on each fillet. Quickly sauté the sliced garlic in the hot pan for 1–2 minutes to brown, adding a squeeze of fresh lemon and butter to finish. Swirl the pan around to melt the butter, then spoon the sauce over the fillets and garnish with fresh parsley leaves.

chef's note

I love the slate-green, small Le Puy lentils, grown in the Le Puy region of France. Because of their unique flavor, they are considered to be the best lentil, and they hold their shape during cooking. Simply cook the lentils in a pan of simmering water for 20 minutes, or until tender, then drain them. Heat a few tablespoons of extra virgin olive oil in a clean pan, add some chopped onion, garlic, and green chile, then add the cooked lentils to heat through and finish with a squeeze of fresh lemon juice, seasoning with salt, pepper, and fresh cilantro.

GOOD FRIDAY FISH WITH CRISPY DILL

This perfect summer food is super quick and super easy. This is my adapted version of the recipe inspired by Donna Hay, the go-to girl for quick and simple meals. Switch it up by adding capers or even changing out the lemon with orange or lime zest. This pairs beautifully with a chilled bottle of oaked Chardonnay, Viognier, or Sauvignon Blanc.

SERVES 4

For the fish

4 tablespoons butter

2 tablespoons extra virgin olive oil

4 garlic cloves, sliced thick

1 small serrano chile, seeds removed and chopped

4 (6-ounce) firm white fish fillets, seabass or halibut

Freshly ground pepper and sea salt

For the crispy dill

4 tablespoons extra virgin olive oil

1 cup dill sprigs

2 tablespoons lemon zest

Lemon wedges

Heat a large, nonstick frying pan over medium-low heat.

Add 2 tablespoons butter and 1 tablespoon olive oil, and sauté the garlic and chile, stirring occasionally for 2–3 minutes, or until soft. Set aside. Wipe out the pan. Heat 2 more tablespoons butter and 1 tablespoon olive oil in the same pan, increase the heat to medium, sprinkle the fish with salt and a few grinds of pepper, and cook for 3–4 minutes on each side, or until cooked through. Remove the fish to a serving platter.

Heat 4 tablespoons olive oil in a small frying pan over medium heat and fry the dill sprigs in small batches. Be careful, as they only take one minute or so to crisp. Remove the fried dill onto paper towels. Top the fish with the sliced garlic and serrano chile, crispy dill, and lemon zest, and serve with lemon wedges.

PARMESAN-CRUSTED CHICKEN

Most kids are hooked on breaded chicken of some sort. Here's a pan-fried version that's much healthier than frozen options or a drive-through. It's extra crispy and delicious, always a crowd favorite—and not just for kids!

SERVES 4

4 (6-ounce) organic chicken breasts, boneless and skinless

2 eggs, beaten

¼ cup Dijon mustard

1 garlic clove, minced

2 cups panko bread crumbs

½ cup grated Parmesan cheese

3 tablespoons minced fresh parsley

1 teaspoon sea salt

¼ teaspoon freshly ground pepper

Vegetable oil

Wash and pat dry the chicken and cut in strips if you like.

Whisk the eggs, mustard, and garlic together in a shallow dish.

In another shallow dish, mix together the bread crumbs, Parmesan cheese, parsley, salt, and pepper. Dip both sides of the chicken in the egg mixture, coating it well. Quickly place the chicken in the bread crumbs, and toss the crumbs over the edges and top of the chicken breasts, using your hands to press the chicken into the crumbs to make them stick. Turn the chicken over and again press into the crumbs. Set finished pieces aside and repeat with all the chicken pieces.

Preheat the oven to 350°F. Heat a large skillet over medium-high heat and sauté a few pieces at a time in a small amount of oil to brown the chicken, 2–3 minutes on each side, removing the browned pieces to a baking pan. Bake all the pieces together in the oven for 35–40 minutes and serve warm.

chef's note
Be sure to use finely grated Parmesan cheese, as shredded cheese won't stick to the chicken quite as well.

"Wine makes daily living easier,
less hurried, with fewer tensions
and more tolerance."

—BENJAMIN FRANKLIN
(1706-1790)

grapes notes

Thyme-Roasted Grapes

Pickled Grapes

Roasted Squash and Warm Farro with Slow-Roasted Grapes

Roasted Cauliflower with Warm Bacon Dressing

Smoked Turkey Waldorf Salad

Wine Harvest Grilled Pizza

Hot Pepper-Infused Oil

Spicy Maple Grape-Glazed Salmon

Pork Chops with Dried Fruit

Sausage and Grapes

Fall Harvest Roasted Chicken

Seared Duck Breast with Spicy Grape Sauce

Grilled Lamb Medallions with Grape Glaze

Grape Focaccia

Spanish Grape Tart

Grape Salsa

THYME-ROASTED GRAPES

Roasting grapes, with a little help from a drizzle of olive oil, a hint of fresh thyme, and a touch of salt and pepper, brings out their natural juices. I use these roasted caramelized grapes in many recipes in this book. Try adding them to your next cheese board, toss them into a grain salad or with some roasted sausages, or use them as a topping on focaccia. The possibilities are endless and delicious.

———— **MAKES 4 CUPS** ————

2 pounds seedless grapes (red, green, or black), washed and drained

Small handful fresh thyme sprigs

3 tablespoons extra virgin olive oil

Freshly ground pepper and sea salt

Preheat the oven to 425°F.

Set the washed grapes on a parchment paper-lined baking pan (on or off the stem, it's up to you). Scatter the thyme sprigs around, then drizzle with the olive oil and sprinkle with salt and pepper. Toss everything around a bit, making sure the grapes are well-coated with the oil.

Roast until the grapes have caramelized in spots and are starting to burst, 30 minutes or so, shaking and rotating the pan once or twice during roasting. Let cool slightly before using.

Once completely cooled, refrigerate any leftover grapes in an airtight container for 2–3 days.

PICKLED GRAPES

Preserves like jams, chutneys and pickles, which seem to multiply in my refrigerator, often find their way to my table, since I was raised with the notion that dinner does not have to include a protein, starch, and a green vegetable. Along with a couple of wedges of cheese, some crisp crackers or a hunk of bread, these grapes make a feast served on a worn wooden board I keep for just this sort of meal. Eating a meal of small bites after a busy day, with a glass of wine, is liberating and a fun way to connect with family and friends. Scatter these pickles on salads or, as I do, eat them straight from the jar. If you haven't eaten pickled grapes, I seriously urge you try a batch. I like these made with cinnamon and black pepper and have also made them with rosemary and chile. Whichever flavor combination you choose, be sure to use fresh grapes, cleaned and washed well. Keep the whole batch for yourself in one quart-size jar or split it into smaller jars to give as gifts.

MAKES 1 QUART

1 pound red grapes

1 cup apple cider vinegar

¼ cup filtered water

1 cup granulated white sugar

1 cinnamon stick

½ vanilla bean

¼ teaspoon whole cloves

¼ teaspoon whole black peppercorns

⅛ teaspoon yellow mustard seeds

First wash the grapes well.

In a small saucepan, combine the vinegar, water, and sugar, and bring to a boil over high heat for a few minutes. Place the spices at the bottom of a 1-quart jar.

Add the grapes to the jar on top of the spices, then pour the hot vinegar into the jar over the grapes. Let the grapes sit until cool. Place a lid on the jar and refrigerate, or follow proper canning procedures. Let the pickled grapes marinate in the fridge for at least 24 hours before serving.

ROASTED SQUASH AND WARM FARRO WITH SLOW-ROASTED GRAPES

Usher in fall with some of the season's finest fruits and vegetables. Chewy farro—an Italian whole grain—is tossed with roasted squash and mixed greens in this colorful salad. It's flavored by grapes that have been slow roasted in a low-temperature oven to concentrate their sweetness and release their juices.

SERVES 4–6

2 cups seedless red grapes

Extra virgin olive oil

1 pound squash, butternut or kabocha, peeled, cut into 1-inch cubes

2 small red onions, sliced into ½-inch wedges

1 tablespoon red wine vinegar

2 tablespoons fresh rosemary, chopped fine

Freshly ground pepper and sea salt

2 cups cooked farro, or another grain

Mixed greens, such as baby kale, chard, red mustard, or arugula

Toasted nuts or seeds, pistachio, sunflower, and/or pumpkin seeds

Preheat the oven to 300°F.

Arrange the grapes in a single layer on a parchment paper-lined baking sheet. Drizzle lightly with olive oil and slow roast the grapes for about an hour, until they have shrunk to about half their size, and are still juicy. Set aside to cool.

On another parchment paper-lined baking sheet, toss the cubed squash and red onion wedges with olive oil, red wine vinegar, rosemary, ½ teaspoon salt, and a few grinds of pepper and spread out evenly. Roast at 400°F for about 30 minutes, until lightly browned at the edges.

When ready to serve, combine the cooked farro in a large mixing bowl with the roasted grapes, roasted squash and onions, and toss gently with the mixed baby greens. Add a pinch or two of salt and a few grinds of pepper before serving.

Arrange the salad on a platter and garnish with chopped nuts or seeds to add to the crunchy texture.

chef's note

Farro, an ancient grain, has been eaten for thousands of years around the world, and it is beginning to gain traction for its health benefits and ability to adapt to different recipes. Similar to kamut or bulgur wheat, and high in fiber, farro makes a good alternative grain addition to many dishes. While it does contain gluten, the levels are lower than in today's wheat because the gluten is broken down by sprouting and fermentation, similar to the sourdough process. Farro can be much more tolerable for anyone sensitive to gluten. Farro is available in Mediterranean or Middle Eastern markets, and if you can't find it, you certainly can substitute other ancient grains, like brown or wild rice, quinoa, or spelt.

ROASTED CAULIFLOWER WITH WARM BACON DRESSING

My latest cooking obsession is roasted cauliflower. It's low maintenance, low carb, and gluten free, and in this recipe the edges get all browned and caramelized. Roasted, the cauliflower tastes nutty and buttery, without any added nuts or butter. I knew this salad would be great by combining my favorite vegetable with roasted grapes, and, of course, as the saying goes, bacon makes everything better. This can be served as a side dish, or it works well as a satisfying meal at lunchtime.

SERVES 4–6

1 head cauliflower, cut into bite-size florets

½ pound red grapes, stemmed and halved, about 1 ½ cups

2 garlic cloves, sliced

1 teaspoon fresh thyme leaves

¼ cup extra virgin olive oil

Freshly ground pepper and sea salt

½ cup toasted nuts, pistachios or walnuts, crushed

Preheat the oven to 400°F. On a paper-lined baking pan toss the cauliflower with the stemmed grapes, sliced garlic, thyme leaves, and olive oil with 1 teaspoon of salt and a few grinds of pepper. Roast for 30–40 minutes, until the cauliflower is tender and caramelized, stirring halfway through.

Transfer to a serving platter, drizzle with some of the warm bacon dressing and sprinkle with some crushed nuts.

BACON DRESSING

MAKES ABOUT 1½ CUPS

1 tablespoon grapeseed oil

½ cup red onion, chopped fine

6 slices of bacon, diced

⅓ cup apple cider vinegar

2 teaspoons Dijon mustard

⅔ cup extra virgin olive oil

½ teaspoon sea salt

Freshly ground pepper

1 teaspoon chives, snipped

Heat the grapeseed oil in a small pan over medium heat and fry the onion and bacon for 4–5 minutes, until the bacon is crispy. Transfer to a small bowl and whisk in the vinegar, mustard, and olive oil. Season with salt and a few grinds of pepper and finish with the chives. Serve warm over the salad or reheat later for other uses.

chef's note
The mild onion-like flavor of chives complements a variety of dishes, making it a versatile choice for your home herb garden. Using kitchen scissors, finely snip the chives into small pieces. Alternatively, use a very sharp chef's knife to cut the chives into slices.

SMOKED TURKEY WALDORF SALAD

Based on the original Waldorf salad created at New York City's famed Waldorf-Astoria Hotel, this simple, yet flavorful, version is a bit healthier with the addition of smoked turkey and the substitution of part of the mayonnaise in the dressing with nonfat yogurt. The salad still keeps all of its great texture and crunch. If you are a sandwich lover like me, pile it on thick toasted bread or rolls for a perfect picnic take-along.

SERVES 4–6

2 tart green apples, cut into 1-inch dice

2 tablespoons fresh lemon juice

¼ cup dried cranberries

½ cup mayonnaise

½ cup nonfat plain yogurt

2 tablespoons blue cheese (optional)

1 tablespoon honey

½ teaspoon sea salt

Freshly ground pepper

1 cup smoked turkey breast, cut into 1-inch cubes

1 cup red seedless grapes, sliced in half

1 cup walnut pieces, toasted

1 cup celery (about 3 stalks), sliced thin

2 green onions, sliced thin

Pinch of cayenne pepper

1 head butter lettuce, washed

Bread or rolls

In a large bowl, toss the cut apples with the lemon juice and set aside.

In a smaller bowl, cover the cranberries with boiling water to soften, 3–5 minutes, then drain well. For the dressing, combine the mayonnaise, yogurt, blue cheese if you like, honey, salt, and a few grinds of pepper and stir until smooth. Add other spices or fresh-cut herbs.

Add the softened cranberries, smoked turkey, grapes, walnuts, celery, and green onion to the apples. Pour the dressing over the mixture and toss gently until all ingredients are evenly coated.

To serve, arrange the salad on top of lettuce leaves or on bread or rolls.

chef's note
As a variation, try adding a touch of curry powder, coriander, or turmeric for added color and flavor. Add brightness to the dish with fresh herbs from the garden, like tarragon, chives, or cilantro.

WINE HARVEST GRILLED PIZZA

Grilled pizza crust is topped with roasted grapes and can be enjoyed in any season as an appetizer or main course. If you are lucky enough to be in wine country during grape harvest, look for ripe grapes straight off the vine. The flavor of this topping, a savory blend of sweet and sour known as *agrodolce*, popular in Mediterranean cooking, is offset by the saltiness and richness of the prosciutto.

SERVES 2–4

12 ounces pizza dough
(see recipe, page 114) or
use pre-made pizza dough

Pizza topping
(see recipe, page 113)

6 tablespoons extra virgin
olive oil

8 slices prosciutto

Coarse sea salt and
freshly ground pepper

Prepare a wood or charcoal fire or preheat a gas grill, with the grill rack set 3–4 inches above the heat. Divide the dough into 2 balls, roll each into a 6-inch, free-form circle and place onto an oiled, inverted baking pan. Spread and flatten the dough with your hands into a larger 10-inch form. You may end up with a rectangle rather than a circle—the shape is unimportant—but be sure to maintain even thickness. Make the other piece into another large shape.

When the fire is hot (or the gas grill has been preheated), use your fingertips to lift the dough gently by the two corners closest to you and quickly drape the dough onto the hot grill rack. Within a minute or so, the dough will puff up slightly, the underside will start to cook and grill marks will appear. Using tongs, immediately flip the crust over and grill just briefly on the other side, removing to a sheet pan after a minute. Repeat with the second piece, then brush each crust with 1 tablespoon olive oil, spread with half the onion-grape filling, and top with 4 slices of prosciutto. Drizzle with olive oil. Turn the heat on your grill down to low. Slide or place the pizza back onto the grill. With your tongs, rotate the pizza around to finish cooking, checking the underside to make sure it is not burning. As the onion mixture heats through, the prosciutto on top will warm up as well.

Transfer to a wood board, sprinkle with coarse sea salt and a few grinds of pepper, cut, and serve with hot-pepper infused oil.

FOR THE TOPPING

3 tablespoons extra virgin
   olive oil

3 large onions, peeled,
   sliced thin

¼ cup red wine vinegar

1 cup roasted grapes, chopped
   rough (see recipe, page 102)

1 cinnamon stick

¼ teaspoon crushed fennel seed

1 teaspoon sea salt

1 cup water

Heat a large skillet over medium heat, add the olive oil and
sauté the onions, stirring occasionally, for about 20 minutes,
until the onions are very soft and brown. Stir in the vinegar
and allow to reduce. Add the roasted grapes, cinnamon stick,
fennel, salt, and water. Bring to a boil, then lower the heat to
a simmer and stew for 10–15 minutes, stirring occasionally.
Allow the mixture to reduce to the consistency of loose jam.
Remove the cinnamon stick.

You can use right away or cool to room temperature and
refrigerate in a covered glass jar for up to a week.

PIZZA DOUGH

MAKES 2 MEDIUM 10-INCH PIZZAS

1 envelope (2 ½ teaspoons)
    active dry yeast

1 cup warm water

Pinch of sugar

2 teaspoons sea salt

¼ cup fine-ground cornmeal

3 tablespoons whole wheat flour

1 tablespoon extra virgin olive oil

2 ½–3 cups unbleached
    white flour

Dissolve the dry yeast in warm water with a pinch of sugar to activate and set aside for 5 minutes. Stir in the salt, cornmeal, whole wheat flour, and oil. Gradually add the white flour, stirring with a wooden spoon until dough forms.

Place the dough on a floured board and knead it for several minutes, until smooth, elastic, and shiny, adding only enough additional flour to keep the dough from sticking to your board.

Transfer to a lightly oiled bowl, turn the dough to coat with oil and cover with a dry towel.

Allow the dough to rise in a warm place until double in size, about 1 hour.

Punch down the dough and knead once more. Let the dough rise again for 45 minutes.

After this somewhat long process, your dough is now ready to be made into pizza! Punch down the dough, and get ready to roll it out, or divide into small balls, wrap up, and refrigerate until ready to use. Allow the dough to come to room temperature before using.

HOT PEPPER-INFUSED OIL

While living in Spain, we often ate pizza at a local pizzeria in our little village of Monda. When we asked for chiles, while I pantomimed sprinkling with my fingers, they gave us an inquisitive look. It turned out they never used dried chile flakes. Instead, a fragrant infusion of garlic and chile was prepared weekly and served in a beautiful, delicate, green Spanish glass bottle with a very fragile glass spout. You will love this oil, and it will quickly become one of your favorite new condiments.

MAKES 2 CUPS

2 cups extra virgin olive oil

2 tablespoons hot
   Hungarian paprika

2 tablespoons chile flakes

2 garlic cloves, peeled

Combine all the ingredients in a heavy saucepan and bring slowly to a boil over medium heat. Turn the heat down to very low and gently simmer for 15 minutes. Remove from the heat and set aside for 30 minutes. The flavors will continue to infuse the oil as it cools. Strain the oil into a clean glass bottle or jar. The chile-infused oil will keep for a few days at room temperature or in the fridge for at least 2 weeks. Great as an alternative to dried chile flakes!

SPICY MAPLE GRAPE-GLAZED SALMON

This spicy grape glaze requires only a few ingredients and you wouldn't believe how amazing it tastes! Heart-healthy salmon seared and bathed in the lime-infused glaze makes for an easy and delicious weekday dinner.

──────── **SERVES 4** ────────

2 cups grapes, washed and stemmed

3 garlic cloves, chopped

¼ cup maple syrup

2 limes, zested and juiced

2 tablespoons hot sauce

Pinch of cayenne

½ teaspoon sea salt

4 (6-oz) salmon fillets, skin removed

Grapeseed oil

Prepare the glaze by blending the grapes, garlic, maple syrup, half of the lime zest and ¼ cup lime juice, hot sauce, and cayenne together in a blender. Add salt and blend until smooth. Strain if you used grapes with seeds. Then pour into a small sauté pan set over medium heat and simmer until the mixture is reduced to a glaze. Set aside. Save half of the lime zest for garnish.

Preheat the oven to 400°F.

Brush the salmon fillets lightly with the grapeseed oil and sprinkle lightly with salt.

Heat a large oven-safe nonstick pan over high heat until very hot and place the salmon in the pan, top side down. Sear on one side for a few minutes, till golden brown, gently flip over, remove from heat, and generously spoon the spicy maple-grape glaze over the salmon. Slide the pan into the preheated oven and roast the salmon until just cooked through, 5–7 minutes. Remove from the oven and baste with the pan juices.

Plate the salmon and garnish with reserved lime zest and extra glaze, if you like.

chef's note
I have also made this glaze with leftover roasted grapes, which gives it a more concentrated grape flavor—both methods are equally good. When zesting the lime, add a bit of water to the reserved zest for garnish to prevent the zest from drying out. Grilling the salmon works as well for this recipe. Brush on the glaze during the last few minutes of grilling, careful not to let the glaze burn.

PORK CHOPS WITH DRIED FRUIT

When I was playing with this pairing of pork chops with dried fruit, I was happy to see the apricots and prunes plumped up during roasting, and added a nice fruitiness that went so well with the grapes, garlic, and sage—and the pork was perfectly tender. The combination was irresistible!

———————— **SERVES 6** ————————

6 bone-in thick pork chops, 10-12 ounces each

6 tablespoons extra virgin olive oil

Freshly ground pepper and sea salt

3 cups red seedless grapes

1 cup dried fruit, peaches, apricots, or prunes

½ cup caramelized garlic cloves (see recipe below)

½ cup fresh sage leaves, divided

3 small red onions, peeled and cut in half

½ cup red wine

Remove the pork chops from the refrigerator and let sit at room temperature for about 20 minutes. Position a rack in the upper third of your oven and preheat to 400°F.

Rub the chops with 3 tablespoons of olive oil and sprinkle generously with salt and pepper.

In a bowl, toss together the grapes and dried fruit, the remaining 3 tablespoons olive oil, caramelized garlic, and half of the sage leaves. Sprinkle lightly with salt and pepper and set aside.

Sear the red onion halves in a large pan on top of the stove until well caramelized on one side, and set aside. In the same pan, sear the pork chops over medium-high heat to brown both sides very well, then place the chops in an oven-safe baking dish, top with the grape mixture, and arrange the onion halves in with the chops. Add the red wine to the dish and roast about 20 minutes, until the chops are done and the grapes are starting to burst. Let rest for 5 minutes, transfer the chops to a serving platter with the fruit and onions, and drizzle with the pan juices. Garnish with fresh sage leaves.

CARAMELIZED GARLIC

2 cups peeled garlic cloves

1 ½ cups balsamic vinegar

½ cup extra virgin olive oil

Combine the peeled garlic with the balsamic vinegar and olive oil in a heavy saucepan and spread out in one layer. Bring the liquid to a boil, then reduce the heat to low and simmer gently for about 20 minutes, until the garlic is very soft and the vinegar has become syrupy. Set aside to cool. The mixture will thicken up more once cooled. Use these little morsels in recipes, serve them on your cheese board or antipasti platter with cured meats, or add to salad dressings. The garlic can be stored in the fridge for up to a week.

SAUSAGE AND GRAPES

This dish was inspired by a recipe in the *Zuni Cafe Cookbook* by Judy Rogers. It is truly a hearty celebration dish for autumn, when grapes are at their peak. Prepared with a good Italian fennel sausage and plated with stone-ground cornmeal polenta or creamy, cheesy grits that can capture the syrupy grape pan juices, this dish is quite easy to concoct, making it a perfect weeknight dinner.

SERVES 4

1 tablespoon extra virgin olive oil

6 large Italian or chicken sausages

½ cup low-sodium chicken broth

1 small red onion, chopped fine

1 pound seedless grapes

2 sprigs fresh rosemary

½ cup dry white wine

2 tablespoons fresh parsley, chopped

Preheat the oven to 450°F. Heat a large cast iron or heavy skillet over high heat. Add the olive oil and sausages, and brown the sausages on both sides for about 5 minutes. Add the broth, chopped onion, grapes, and rosemary sprigs to the pan and put in the oven for 20 minutes, turning the sausages and grapes halfway through, until the sausages are cooked and the grapes begin to burst and caramelize. Remove only the sausages onto a serving dish.

In the same roasting pan, over medium-high heat on the stovetop, carefully pour in the wine, and stir until the wine is reduced, scraping up the browned bits at the bottom of the pan into the roasted grapes. Pour the thickened pan juices, along with the grapes, over the sausages.

Garnish with the chopped parsley.

FALL HARVEST ROASTED CHICKEN

We are all on an endless search for a new and different way to prepare roast chicken. It's the meal you "enthusiastically" construct to satisfy those you feed day after day, only to get a reluctant—"it's good"—as your only feedback. Why not jazz up the occasion by spicing up your weekly bird with fennel, cumin, and coriander, harmonized with grapes, black olives, and a splash of white wine?

_____ SERVES 4–6 _____

3 pounds bone-in, skin-on whole chicken, cut into parts (thighs, drumsticks, and/or breasts)

Freshly ground pepper and sea salt

1 teaspoon ground fennel

1 teaspoon ground cumin

1 teaspoon ground coriander

2 tablespoons extra virgin olive oil

1 cup seedless grapes

1 cup Kalamata olives, pitted

2 shallots, peeled, sliced thin

½ cup dry white wine

½ cup chicken broth or water

Preheat the oven to 400°F.

Wash and pat the chicken dry, then season generously with salt, pepper, and the fennel, cumin, and coriander.

Heat a heavy, ovenproof 12-inch skillet (cast iron works best) over medium-high heat. Working in batches, take your time browning the chicken pieces on both sides in olive oil, transferring the first batch to a plate, while the second batch browns nicely again on both sides. Return all the chicken pieces to the pan, skin side up, and surround with the grapes, pitted olives, and shallots. Roast the chicken in the oven for about 45 minutes, until cooked through and the juices run clear.

Transfer the chicken to a platter, leaving the grapes and olives in the skillet. Place on the stovetop over medium-high heat, and carefully add the wine and chicken broth or water to the skillet. Bring to a boil, scraping up any browned bits, and cook for 2–3 minutes, until reduced by half. Pour the sauce, grapes and all, over the chicken to serve.

SEARED DUCK BREAST WITH SPICY GRAPE SAUCE

When I first moved to Spain, almost 18 years ago, I didn't have a tremendous amount of experience cooking duck, though, to my surprise, I found duck breasts to be very plentiful there and surprisingly reasonably-priced. My private clients from England requested I make duck, sometimes two days in a row. Sweet grapes reduced in red wine and luxurious, fatty duck breasts—this is a fancy dinner that kids and grown-ups all love.

SERVES 4

2 tablespoons unsalted butter

1 tablespoon extra virgin olive oil

4 tablespoons onion, chopped fine

3 cloves roasted garlic, chopped fine

2 teaspoons fresh jalapeño, minced

½ cup port wine

1 cup red wine

1 cup chicken broth

1 cup Concord grape juice, fresh or bottled

1 cup seedless black grapes, halved

Freshly ground pepper and sea salt

4 (7-ounce) Muscovy duck breasts

In a medium saucepan over medium-high heat, melt the butter with olive oil and sauté the onion, garlic, and jalapeño for about 5 minutes. Raise the heat to high, add the port and red wine, and reduce to half a cup. Add the chicken broth and grape juice and reduce by half, then turn the heat down to low, stir in the grapes, and cook for a few minutes with ½ teaspoon salt and a generous amount of freshly ground pepper.

Pat the duck breasts dry and score the fat a couple of times in two directions to create a crosshatch pattern, cutting through the fat but not into the meat. Sprinkle each breast generously with salt and a few grinds of pepper.

Preheat the oven to 375°F. Preheat a large ovenproof skillet on high heat, until smoking. Place the duck breasts in the pan, fatty skin side down, and adjust the heat to medium so it doesn't burn. Sear the breasts for 6–8 minutes, until the fat has been rendered. Pour off most of the fat, turn the breasts over, place them in the oven and cook for about 10 minutes for medium-rare doneness. Remove the duck from the pan and let rest for 5 minutes. To serve, cut each breast into six or seven thin slices and brush liberally with the spicy grape sauce.

GRILLED LAMB MEDALLIONS WITH GRAPE GLAZE

When I was growing up in a Jewish household, lamb was traditionally served every year at our Passover meal. The smell of the roasting meat wafting through the house all day, honestly, was not that appealing to me. In this recipe, outdoor grilling significantly cuts down on the cooking time, and the aroma of the charred meat curling up from the grill is much more pleasing. The perfectly grilled lamb, brushed with the honey-chile-infused grape glaze, is a mouthwatering combination!

SERVES 6–8

2 tablespoons extra virgin olive oil

2 shallots, peeled and sliced

4 garlic cloves, sliced

4 cups black grapes, Concord

3 tablespoons balsamic vinegar

2 tablespoons honey

¼ cup red wine

½ cup chicken broth

2 bay leaves

Pinch of chile flakes, optional

Freshly ground pepper and sea salt

7–8 pounds boneless leg of lamb, trimmed, cut into medallions for grilling

¼ cup green onion, green and white parts, cut in long strips

¼ cup toasted almonds, chopped rough

Add the olive oil, sliced shallots, and garlic to a medium saucepan, and sauté over medium heat, about 3 minutes, until soft and very fragrant. Add the grapes, vinegar, honey, red wine, chicken broth, bay leaves, a pinch of salt, and chile flakes. (Experiment with different spices to shift the flavor.) Reduce the heat and cook the mixture until the grapes burst open and the sauce has reduced down to a glaze. Remove from the heat. Since Concord grapes have thick skins and seeds, pass the glaze through a mesh strainer. If using seedless grapes, the sauce may not need to be strained. Taste and adjust the seasoning with more salt and pepper, as needed.

Brush the glaze onto the lamb medallions toward the end of the grilling time, so it caramelizes a bit but doesn't burn.

Serve the grilled lamb with slivers of sliced green onion and chopped almonds for garnish, with additional glaze on the side.

chef's note
Experiment with different flavors and optional spices—curry powder or toasted cumin seeds for an Indian taste, spicy harissa for a Moroccan flavor, or simply add fresh chopped rosemary for a Tuscan spin. The black grape glaze also complements the flavor of turkey, and is amazing on duck as well. Rack of lamb is also a great option. Brush the meat with the glaze 3 or 4 minutes before it is finished grilling or roasting. You can make the glaze up to 2 days before using; if storing, use within a week.

GRAPE FOCACCIA

Almost every time I go to San Francisco, I explore and shop in Little Italy. Nestled in North Beach, it is one of the most tourist-friendly neighborhoods in the city. When there, I always visit Liguria Bakery, the classic Italian storefront doling out handmade focaccia. The lines are out the door, so it's important to get the focaccia first thing before they sell out. Ambrogio Soracco, the founding father, brought the secret recipe over from Genoa, and the family has been baking and selling their famous focaccia since 1911. Making my interpretation of this versatile flatbread, I bake it with grapes, onions, and walnuts, perfumed by earthy rosemary.

MAKES 1 MEDIUM FOCACCIA

1 cup warm water

2 teaspoons sugar

1 tablespoon active dry yeast

3 cups all-purpose flour, divided

3 tablespoons extra virgin olive oil, plus extra for pan

1 teaspoon fresh rosemary, chopped fine

2 teaspoons sea salt

2 tablespoons coarse cornmeal or semolina, for the pan

For the topping

2 tablespoons extra virgin olive oil, plus more for brushing

1 medium onion, halved lengthwise and sliced thin

1 teaspoon crushed fennel seeds

1 teaspoon sea salt

1 teaspoon freshly ground pepper

2 cups grapes, washed and halved

1 cup walnuts, chopped

2 teaspoons sugar for top

Pour the water into a large bowl, add the sugar, sprinkle the yeast on top, and stir well. After 5 minutes or so, when small bubbles start to form, add 1 ½ cups of flour and stir well to make a sponge. Cover and let rest in a warm spot for 10 minutes to activate the yeast. Add another 1 ½ cups of flour, olive oil, chopped rosemary, and salt, and stir until a mass of dough forms.

Place the dough into an oiled, clean bowl, cover, and set aside for 30 minutes.

Heat 2 tablespoons of olive oil in a large sauté pan over medium heat and sauté the sliced onions seasoned with the crushed fennel, salt, and pepper, for about 5 minutes, until lightly browned. Then toss in the grapes and stir for a few minutes to release the grape juices. Set aside to cool.

On a well-floured work surface, turn out the dough and sprinkle with a few tablespoons of flour. Gently knead the dough until it is smooth, about 5 minutes, adding as little flour as possible. Cover and set aside to rest and rise for another 30 minutes or so. Preheat the oven to 450°F. Generously brush an 18 x 13-inch baking sheet with olive oil and sprinkle with the cornmeal. Place the dough on the pan and, with oiled hands, press out into a rectangle. This does not need to be perfectly shaped. Lightly drizzle with more olive oil on top and dimple the dough all over with your fingertips. Cover the dough with cooled sautéed onions and grapes within half an inch of the edges, and scatter the chopped walnuts over the top. Sprinkle lightly with sugar. Bake the dough about 25 minutes, until golden brown.

Serve warm or at room temperature.

SPANISH GRAPE TART

In Spain, it's thought that eating one grape with every strike of the clock at midnight brings good luck for the New Year. A dozen grapes is definitely more than a mouthful, trust me, I tried it while living in Andalucia many moons ago. This grape tart, however, gives you all 12 grapes in just a few sweet bites.

SERVES 8

1 pound red or green seedless grapes, washed and stemmed

¼ cup sugar

For the pastry

2 cups unbleached white flour

1 teaspoon sea salt

8 tablespoons unsalted butter, chilled and cut into pieces

2 tablespoons ice water

2 eggs, lightly beaten

¼ cup crème fraîche

2 tablespoons sugar

Prick the grapes with a fork and place in a large bowl. Add sugar and mix well. Cover and set aside to macerate at room temperature for about 3 hours.

For the pastry, combine the flour and salt in a large bowl. Cut in the chilled butter with a pastry cutter or 2 knives, until the mixture resembles coarse crumbs. Add 2 tablespoons of ice water, one spoonful at a time, and mix until the dough holds together. Form into a flat disk, wrap in plastic wrap, and refrigerate for at least 1 hour.

Preheat the oven to 350°F. Roll the dough into a 12-inch round on a well-floured surface. Place into a 9-inch tart pan with a removeable bottom. Trim the edges, allowing a ½-inch overhang, then fold over and crimp. Drain the macerated grapes and scatter them in a single layer on top of the pastry. Bake about 40 minutes, until the crust begins to color.

Mix together the eggs and crème fraîche in a small bowl. Pour the mixture evenly over the grapes and continue baking about 10 more minutes, until the filling begins to set. Sprinkle 2 tablespoons of sugar on top and bake about another 10 minutes, until the filling is lightly browned.

Cool slightly before serving.

chef's note
I love the savory notes of rosemary and lavender with grapes. Try adding 1 teaspoon of chopped rosemary or 1 teaspoon of crushed dried lavender to this pastry, or use a ½ teaspoon each mixed together for an herb-infused tart crust.

GRAPE SALSA

Sweet and colorful grapes create a simple and spicy condiment in minutes. Juicy grapes have a similar texture to tomatoes, and the addition of sweet red onion, lime juice, and other herbs and spices makes for a surprisingly tasty and unusual salsa. While grapes may seem like an unlikely partner for fish dishes, one of the first French fish recipes I learned to prepare, oh, so many years ago in culinary school, was Sole Veronique, an entrée where grapes play a starring role. Try this as a topping with mild fish or as a unique salsa with fish tacos.

─── **MAKES 2 CUPS** ───

2 tablespoons red onion, chopped fine

1 cup seedless green grapes, quartered

1 cup seedless red grapes, quartered

1 tablespoon fresh lime juice

½ teaspoon red wine vinegar

1 teaspoon jalapeño, chopped fine

¼ teaspoon chile flakes

2 tablespoons cilantro, chopped fine

Freshly ground pepper and sea salt

Your favorite hot sauce, optional

Prep and chop all the ingredients. Stir together the onion and the green and red grapes with the additional items until combined.

Taste and adjust the seasoning, adding another pinch of salt and a splash of hot sauce as needed. Refrigerate for several hours to let the flavors build.

Serve or store in a glass container for up to 3 days.

"Wine is sunlight, held together by water."

—GALILEO GALILEI
(1564-1642)

with red wine

Lamb Shanks with Figs
and Rosemary

Blue Cheese and Pear-Stuffed
Pork Tenderloin

Syrah-Braised Short Ribs

Slow-Roasted Pork Ribs with
Spicy Mango Sauce

Wild Mushroom and Onion
Shepherdless Pie

Chimichurri

Fresh Tomato Pasta Puttanesca

Upside-Down Sweet
Onion Cornbread

Spiced Wine and
Orange Marmalade

LAMB SHANKS WITH FIGS AND ROSEMARY

I ordered the lamb one night at dinner in the port town of Mykonos—slow roasted lamb shanks, meltingly tender and braised in red wine. All I could say was, "We will be doing this again very soon for a dinner party!" If you've never had braised lamb shanks before, you're missing out on one of life's great pleasures. This hearty dish has a sweetness that comes from dried figs and could definitely stand in for comfort food on a chilly night. It's not necessarily something for every day, but it's perfect for a dinner party or a special occasion because it can be made ahead, which I suggest. Making it the day before allows you to chill the sauce so it can be defatted once cold, and the flavors only get better with time, as well.

SERVES 4

4 lamb shanks, trimmed

Freshly ground pepper and sea salt

1 cup unbleached white flour

2 tablespoons extra virgin olive oil

1 large onion, sliced thin

4 garlic cloves, sliced thin

1 cup red wine

2 cups beef broth

1 (14-ounce) can chopped tomatoes

12 dried figs, chopped

1 tablespoon fresh rosemary, chopped

Liberally sprinkle the lamb shanks all over with a mixture of salt and pepper, and dredge in the flour. Heat a large heavy sauce pot over medium-high heat, and brown the shanks in olive oil on all sides. Remove the shanks and set aside.

Sauté the sliced onion and garlic in the pan drippings until soft, about 5 minutes. Add the wine, broth, tomatoes, figs, and rosemary. Return the shanks to the pot and bring the liquid to a boil. Reduce the heat to low, cover and simmer for 1 ½ hours, or cook in a slow cooker for 4–6 hrs.

Remove the shanks and boil the sauce for another 15 minutes or so, until it is reduced to a gravy-like consistency. Taste and adjust the seasoning of the sauce with ½ teaspoon of sea salt and a few grinds of pepper. Put the shanks back in the thickened sauce to heat through until ready to eat.

Serve with fluffy mashed potatoes or buttered egg noodles to sop up all the juices.

BLUE CHEESE AND PEAR-STUFFED PORK TENDERLOIN

Decisions, decisions. The original recipe I found for this dish called for a fig and blue cheese filling; I could not wait to make it. Since I didn't have any dried figs, I substituted a pear, and WOW! The blue cheese worked incredibly well with the roasted pear flavored with rosemary.

─── **SERVES 4–6** ───

2 pork tenderloins (16 ounces)

3 small shallots, peeled and chopped fine

4 garlic cloves, chopped fine

1 teaspoon fresh rosemary, chopped fine

2 firm pears, peeled and cut into ¼-inch cubes

2 tablespoons extra virgin olive oil

1 tablespoon butter

4 ounces blue cheese, crumbled

Freshly ground pepper and sea salt

Kitchen twine for tying

Bring the tenderloins to room temperature about half an hour before cooking.

Heat a large heavy skillet over medium heat, and sauté the shallots and garlic in 1 tablespoon olive oil to lightly brown, about 5 minutes. Add the chopped rosemary and pear cubes, season with 1 teaspoon salt and a few grinds of pepper; stir to combine and warm the pears through. Set aside to cool.

Cut the tenderloins lengthwise down the center of the loin, but do not cut all the way through. Season lightly with salt and pepper on both sides. Stuff the center of each tenderloin with the pear mixture and tie loosely with the twine to hold together.

Preheat the oven to 400°F.

In the same large heavy skillet, brown the meat in 1 tablespoon butter and 1 tablespoon olive oil. Turn during searing to brown all the sides, then place both tenderloins in an ovenproof baking dish and roast in the oven for about 20 minutes. Pull the skillet out of the oven and crumble the blue cheese on top of the stuffing. Put back into the oven and continue roasting another 10–15 minutes. Insert a thermometer into the thickest part of the meat, avoiding the stuffing; it should reach 160°F for medium doneness. Remove the meat from the oven, cover it loosely with foil and let rest for 10 minutes before removing twine and cutting.

Slice and serve warm with roasted vegetables.

SYRAH-BRAISED SHORT RIBS

I am guessing you remember that slow cooker you bought years ago. You just had to have it and then shoved it away in the top cabinet above your oven. Well, it's time to dust it off and try this easy recipe. Once you get all the ingredients together, you can plug in your cooker and have a satisfying, effortless, fall-off-the-bone tender beef short rib dinner ready at the end of your busy day. The flavor combination of the braised ribs, wine sauce, and mashed veggies creates, without a doubt, a delicious, comforting meal to savor and share with a great full-bodied bottle of red wine you have been saving for that special occasion.

SERVES 4

2 teaspoons sea salt, more as needed

1 teaspoon freshly ground pepper

1 teaspoon ground coriander

4 pounds bone-in beef short ribs

1 tablespoon grapeseed oil

3 leeks, white part only, sliced thin

2 large fennel bulbs, sliced thin

4 garlic cloves, sliced

1 tablespoon smoked paprika

1 tablespoon tomato paste

1 cup red wine, Syrah

½ cup pitted prunes, diced

Fennel fronds and/or sliced scallions, for serving

Start by rubbing the salt, pepper, and coriander all over the meat and let it marinate in the refrigerator for an hour or two, or, ideally, overnight.

Heat a large skillet on the stove over medium-high heat and sear the beef in the oil in batches, about 2 minutes per side, until evenly browned on all sides. Transfer the ribs to a plate as the pieces brown. Add the leeks, fennel, and a pinch of salt to the same hot pan and cook until soft, about 8 minutes. Then stir in the garlic, smoked paprika, and tomato paste; cook until fragrant, 1–2 minutes. Pour in the red wine and stir to combine.

Transfer all the sauce ingredients to a slow cooker, along with the short ribs and pitted prunes. Cook on high for 3–4 hours, or low for 6–8 hours. The sauce will reduce to a dark, thick, syrupy consistency and the flavors of the wine will become concentrated and more intense.

Serve over mashed potatoes or mashed root vegetables like parsnips or roasted cauliflower.

SLOW-ROASTED PORK RIBS WITH SPICY MANGO SAUCE

A huge part of making amazing ribs is buying the right kind of meat. I always look for meaty spare ribs for this recipe rather than the typical baby back ribs. Spare ribs are taken from the bottom of the ribs, on the side of the belly of the pig. This is why they are a bigger, meatier, and a little tougher cut of meat. With this slow-roasting method, these ribs come out amazing—if I say so myself. The spicy mango sauce is a great combination of tropical flavors, and the chipotle chile gives this recipe a smoky flavor with a bit of a kick. What to serve with these? Pork spare ribs have no better friend than an earthy, medium-to-full-bodied red wine that will stand up to these bold flavors. Try a Zinfandel, Syrah/Shiraz, Cabernet, Merlot, or Malbec.

―――――――――― **SERVES 4** ――――――――――

2 racks pork spare ribs

Freshly ground pepper
 and sea salt

For the sauce

1 cup sherry

½ cup soy sauce

¼ cup toasted sesame oil

1 cup mango chutney

2 tablespoons honey

2 green onions, white parts,
 chopped

1 tablespoon fresh ginger root,
 chopped

4 garlic cloves, sliced thin

½ teaspoon cayenne pepper

1 teaspoon chipotle
 chile powder

1 teaspoon hot sauce,
 your favorite brand

1 tablespoon fresh lime juice

Green onions, green parts
 sliced thin for garnish

Preheat the oven to 350°F.

Lay the ribs out on two baking pans, rub the meat all over with 2 teaspoons salt and a few grinds of pepper, and place into the preheated oven for 30 minutes.

Meanwhile, blend all the sauce ingredients in a blender.

Reduce the temperature of the oven to 300°F and generously baste the ribs with the sauce every 20 minutes or so. Slowly roast for 2 hours, basting and rotating the pans top to bottom and back to front for uniform cooking.

Serve garnished with raw green onion and extra sauce on the side.

chef's note
If you really love the charred flavor of barbecued ribs, cook the ribs in the oven until the meat is done, then move them to a hot grill for a nice, crusty sear on the outside.

🍃 **chef's note** While mushrooms are a delicious filling, lentils or diced eggplant can stand in as well. You can also prepare this dish in small ramekins as a first course or a simple lunch.

WILD MUSHROOM AND ONION SHEPHERDLESS PIE

While cooking for private clients, I occasionally am asked to prepare vegetarian versions of favorite childhood meals. Traditionally made with leftover roast meat, this veggie twist on a winter classic combines the thick crust of creamy mashed potatoes with a hearty mushroom and caramelized onion ragout, making this the epitome of comfort food that's at least as good as the traditional Irish pub version.

——————— **SERVES 6** ———————

For the potatoes

3 pounds Yukon gold potatoes, peeled and quartered

¼ cup heavy cream

4 tablespoons salted butter

6 tablespoons grated Asiago cheese

1 teaspoon sea salt

Freshly ground pepper

For the mushroom filling

6 tablespoons extra virgin olive oil, divided, plus more for pan

2 medium yellow onions, halved and sliced (3 cups)

3 medium portobello mushrooms

1 ½ pounds assorted wild mushrooms, chopped

1 teaspoon sea salt

Freshly ground pepper

2 garlic cloves, minced

1 cup grated Asiago cheese, plus 2 tablespoons for sprinkling

2 tablespoons chopped herbs, parsley, thyme, and/or sage

To make the potato filling, place the peeled potatoes in a medium pot and add enough cold water to cover them. Add 1 teaspoon of salt and bring to a boil. Then reduce heat to medium-low and simmer 30 minutes, or until just tender. Drain the potatoes—do not rinse with cold water. Warm the cream and butter in a medium pot, careful not to boil the cream, add the drained potatoes, and mash until smooth. Stir in the grated cheese, taste and adjust the seasoning with more salt, if needed. Add a few grinds of pepper, and set aside to cool.

To make the mushroom filling, heat a large skillet over medium heat. Sauté the sliced onions in 2 tablespoons olive oil and cook for 20 minutes, or until golden and caramelized.

While the onions brown, set the portobello mushrooms gill side up on a parchment paper-lined baking pan, drizzle with 1 tablespoon olive oil and roast for 25 minutes in the oven. Let cool and slice thin.

When the onions have caramelized, add the wild mushrooms with the remaining 3 tablespoons olive oil and minced garlic to the pan, season with 1 teaspoon sea salt and a few grinds of pepper, and cook through until the mushrooms are tender. Set aside to cool, then add the cheese and herbs.

Preheat the oven to 375°F.

To set up, brush a 9-inch pie dish with oil. Layer the wild mushroom–onion mixture on the bottom of the pan and follow with a layer of the sliced portobello mushrooms. Top with the potato filling, spreading all the way to the edges. Sprinkle the pie with the grated cheese. Bake 40 minutes, or until golden.

CHIMICHURRI

Chimichurri sauce is an intensely flavored garlic and herb salsa closely related to the open-fire grilling culture of Argentina. Delicious on just about everything, it's a standard condiment for grilled steak. Parsley makes up the bulk of the herbs, with cilantro and basil adding more flavor and brightness. The outstanding taste of chimichurri makes it a flavorful marinade, or simply serve it straight up as a sauce.

MAKES 2 CUPS

1 medium shallot, chopped

3 garlic cloves, minced

1 tablespoon red wine vinegar

1 cup fresh parsley leaves

1 cup fresh basil leaves

½ cup fresh cilantro leaves

1 teaspoon ground cumin

1 teaspoon dried oregano

1 teaspoon smoked paprika

1 teaspoon ground coriander

½ teaspoon chile flakes

1 teaspoon sea salt

1 tablespoon fresh lemon juice

½ cup extra virgin olive oil

Stir together the shallots and garlic in the red wine vinegar and marinate while you pull the herbs from their stems.

In the bowl of a food processor or blender, combine the parsley, basil, and cilantro leaves, add the shallots and garlic with the vinegar, spices, salt, and lemon juice, and pulse to finely chop.

Add the oil in a thin stream with the machine running, stopping to scrape down the sides, and pulsing a few more times to combine. What you want is a rough blend, like a pesto, not a purée. Taste and adjust the seasoning, adding more salt as needed, and maybe another splash of red wine vinegar for more acidity. Store in the refrigerator in an airtight container and use within 1 week.

chef's note

As pictured, chimichurri is best known as an accompaniment to grilled meat. It is also great on grilled vegetables, used as a vinaigrette on grains like farro or wild rice, or spread on toast topped with a fried egg. Simply put—it is a very versatile condiment, good on just about everything.

FRESH TOMATO PASTA PUTTANESCA

I learned how to make a basic pasta sauce when I fled the nest at 17 years old, and this became my go-to, "what should I make for dinner when there is nothing in the house to eat?" Though it's typically made with canned tomatoes, I prefer making this sauce with fresh diced tomatoes. Grape or cherry tomatoes, which are excellent in summer, are among the best tomatoes available year-round. Nothing in this recipe has to be measured precisely, and just a rough chop will do. It's a quick 1-2-3 sauce made while the pasta cooks. We like ours with extra capers and olives and a weekday bottle of red wine.

SERVES 4

2 cups fresh tomatoes

4 garlic cloves

½ cup Kalamata olives

⅓ cup capers, drained

1 tablespoon anchovy paste, optional

½ teaspoon chile flakes

2 tablespoons extra virgin olive oil

Freshly ground pepper and sea salt

Hunk of pecorino or Parmesan

1 pound of your favorite pasta

Prep all the ingredients for your sauce while the pasta is cooking.

Chop the tomatoes by hand or use a food processor to break them down.

Slice the garlic, and pit and chop the olives. Nothing has to be perfect. This is a very rustic sauce.

Heat a heavy-bottomed skillet over medium heat. Sauté the sliced garlic in olive oil with the chile flakes and anchovy paste, if using, for 2 minutes. Add the chopped fresh tomatoes and their juices, olives, and capers. Stir occasionally, bring to a boil, then reduce the heat to low while your pasta is cooking. Because both the capers and olives are salty, as is the cheese, a pinch of salt is all you need, and a few grinds of pepper.

Toss immediately with your favorite pasta cooked al dente. Divide among pasta bowls and grate some fresh Pecorino or Parmesan cheese on each dish.

UPSIDE-DOWN SWEET ONION CORNBREAD

Put your skillet to a new use when you bake this inverted cornbread, adding cheese, orange zest, and pickled jalapeño. To pair, you need a wine with a lot of texture. A California Zinfandel with its mixture of berried fruits, hints of spice, and a generally fruit-forward character, would make a great match for a chili, especially when served with this cornbread.

SERVES 8

1 large or 2 small Vidalia onions

4 tablespoons salted butter

1 cup all-purpose flour

1 cup yellow cornmeal

2 teaspoons sugar

1 tablespoon baking powder

1 teaspoon garlic powder

½ teaspoon sea salt

1 cup ricotta or cottage cheese

1 cup white cheddar cheese, grated

2 eggs

4 ounces (1 stick) salted butter, melted

¼ cup vegetable oil

Zest of 1 orange

1 tablespoon pickled jalapeño slices, diced fine

Preheat the oven to 375°F.

Peel and slice the onions into ½-inch rings, making sure to leave the rings intact.

Heat a large 10-inch cast iron skillet over medium heat and melt the 4 tablespoons butter. Arrange 5–6 large onion ring sections on the bottom of the pan. This will be the top of your "cake." Fill in empty sections with smaller pieces of onion. Sauté the onion rings for 5 minutes, or until softened and starting to caramelize, without disturbing the arrangement.

While the onions are cooking, whisk the flour, cornmeal, sugar, baking powder, garlic powder, and salt together in a large bowl. In a separate smaller bowl, beat the cheeses with the eggs, melted butter, oil, orange zest, and the chopped jalapeño, and stir into dry ingredients until just blended. Do not overmix. Pour the batter over the sautéed onions in the skillet, then transfer the skillet to the oven and bake for 30–35 minutes, or until the cornbread is golden brown and a toothpick inserted into the center comes out clean. Remove from the oven and cool 10–15 minutes.

Carefully invert the cornbread cake onto a serving platter. Slice into wedges and serve with big bowls of chili or simply with a pat of sweet butter and the following Spiced Wine and Orange Marmalade.

chef's note This makes a large amount to share with friends; you can always cut the quantities in half and make a smaller batch for 5–6 jars. Be sure to follow proper shelf-stable canning and sterilization directions to extend the shelf life of your marmalade.

SPICED WINE AND ORANGE MARMALADE

My friend, Maureen (Mo) Foley, from Red Hen Cannery, an artisanal, small-batch jam company based in Santa Barbara, shared this recipe with me. She makes the most delicious and innovative jams and preserves; this marmalade was awarded the bronze medal at the International Dalemain Marmalade Festival in England. Mo was inspired by two things: the need to think of a creative new holiday marmalade, and the memory of her brother's wedding in Sweden, after she tasted *glögg*, the traditional Swedish warm, spiced red wine drink for the first time. Although slightly sweeter than a typical orange-only marmalade, the flavors of the Spiced Wine and Orange Marmalade transform a humble goat cheese or pound cake into a bewitching holiday extravaganza. For a special treat, mix the marmalade with clotted cream and enjoy with your morning scone.

MAKES 12-PLUS, HALF-PINT JARS OF MARMALADE

12 Valencia oranges, approximately 2 ½ pounds

3 cups water

½ cup lemon juice, approximately 4 lemons

4 pounds white sugar

4 ounces red wine

2 teaspoons ground cinnamon

½ teaspoon ground allspice

½ teaspoon ground cardamom

3 whole star anise pods

Plug the sink, place the oranges in it, and fill to cover the oranges with hot water to clean off dirt, wax, or debris. Prepare your food processor with a thin slicing blade. Cut the tops and bottoms of the oranges, then thinly slice in the food processor (or by hand) and add to a large stock pot. Add the water to the oranges and set to a very low simmer for 1 hour. Do not stir. This is a crucial step; do not skip it.

While the oranges and water are simmering, squeeze the lemon juice and add to the orange mix. After an hour of low simmering, add the sugar to the oranges and stir until dissolved. Turn the heat up slightly to a medium simmer. Add the wine and spices and stir until mixed. After 30 minutes or so, check the temperature until the marmalade reads at 220°F. Be patient, this takes awhile, at least an hour or so. Stir regularly with a rubber spatula. If you notice any burning smell before the marmalade reaches temperature, turn down the heat and pour the marmalade into a new pot to continue cooking. When the marmalade reaches 220°F, remove from the stove and cool in the pot for 15 minutes. Fish out the whole star anise pods, then pour into clean jars and cover. Cool the jars for 3–4 hours, then label and place in the fridge, to be stored and consumed within 1 month.

delicious endings

Dark Chocolate Wine Truffles

Upside-Down Berry
Cornmeal Cake

Autumn Fruit Compote with
Lemon Panna Cotta

Grape Crostata with
Ricotta Cream

Pan-Roasted Peaches with
Lavender and Rosemary

Dulce de Leche
(Salted Caramel Sauce)

Farm Stand Fruit Crisp

Grape Granola Bars

Mulled Red Wine Ice Cream

DARK CHOCOLATE WINE TRUFFLES

This may go without saying, but it bears repeating: My thought when pairing wine with chocolate, is that the chocolate should be of the highest quality. Whether the chocolate is white, milk, or dark, its origins should be impeccable. The general rule is the darker the chocolate, the darker the wine. So, reds are ideal for dark chocolate. These decadent wine truffles are infused with red wine, but don't feel constrained. Go ahead and experiment with making milk or white chocolate truffles.

MAKES ABOUT 2 DOZEN TRUFFLES

8 ounces bittersweet chocolate, 60–70% cacao content

½ cup heavy cream

6 tablespoons unsalted butter, cut into small pieces

Pinch of sea salt

½ cup red wine

Raw cacao or cocoa powder

General pairing guidelines

Dark chocolate (50% to 70% cacao content) pairs well with more robust wines, such as Cabernet Sauvignon, Zinfandel, Pinot Noir, and port. A Chianti can be lovely with chocolate around 65% cacao content, while sherry, a fruity Chardonnay, or a sparkling wine will enliven your white chocolate truffles, as these wines will pick up on the buttery, fatty tones of the cocoa butter. Last, but not least, milk chocolate marries well with a Merlot, Pinot Noir, Riesling, and sweeter dessert wines.

Coarsely chop the chocolate and place into a medium-size bowl.

Bring the cream to a simmer, add the butter and stir until melted.

Pour the cream over the chocolate and stir with a spatula until the chocolate is melted.

Add a big pinch of salt and the red wine, and stir until the wine is incorporated.

Pour into an 8 x 8-inch baking dish and refrigerate for at least 4 hours.

For even portions, use a small metal cookie scoop to form each truffle. Coat your hands in cocoa powder and gently roll the chocolate until it forms a uniform ball. Roll in cocoa to coat.

Keep the truffles refrigerated and take them out about 30 minutes before serving.

chef's note
I suggest making these at least a day before eating, to allow the wine flavor to intensify. Keep for up to a week, if they last that long!

UPSIDE-DOWN BERRY CORNMEAL CAKE

This cake is a yearly tradition at my Aunt Janel's Mother's Day brunch, and she shared the recipe with me. A cross between pound cake and cornbread, this cake gets added texture and a bit of crunch from the cornmeal. Piled with fresh berries and a touch of basil and mint, it is simply delicious.

SERVES 10–12

3 cups fresh blueberries, raspberries, and/or blackberries, washed

1 ⅓ cups all-purpose flour

½ cup yellow cornmeal, medium grind

1 tablespoon fresh basil, finely snipped

2 teaspoons baking powder

¼ teaspoon sea salt

2 large eggs, lightly beaten

½ cup sugar

⅔ cup milk (non-dairy milk can be used)

⅓ cup extra virgin olive oil

Fresh basil and mint leaves, sliced thin

Powdered sugar, for garnish

Preheat the oven to 350°F. Lightly butter an 8-inch round cake pan, line the bottom of the pan with parchment paper, and butter the top of the paper. Arrange 2 cups of the mixed berries in the bottom of the pan and set aside.

In a medium bowl, stir together the flour, cornmeal, basil, baking powder, and salt. Set aside.

In another bowl, whisk together the eggs, sugar, milk, and olive oil. Add the egg mixture all at once to the flour mixture. Stir until combined, then pour over the berries and spread evenly.

Bake 40–45 minutes or until a toothpick inserted near the center comes out clean.

Cool the cake in the pan for 5 minutes. Run a knife around the edge of the pan to loosen the sides and invert on your serving plate. Remove the parchment paper.

Top with the remaining cup of fresh berries, tossed with basil and mint, and garnish with a small sprinkling of powdered sugar.

AUTUMN FRUIT COMPOTE WITH LEMON PANNA COTTA

Thinking about harvest and the fall season reminds me of a dish that I often eat as a breakfast treat—dried fruit compote served over yogurt. I use dried fruits from my local farmer's market; simmered with spices, lemon, apples and pears, and a few shots of brandy, they turn into a rich syrupy compote. It is a delicious and slightly decadent way to rehydrate and use the fruits. The compote is so good it can actually be enjoyed by itself; serving it over panna cotta makes it a special dessert.

— SERVES 8 —

2 cups water

1 cup red or white wine

¼ cup packed dark brown sugar

Zest of 1 lemon and 1 orange

2 cinnamon sticks

¼ teaspoon freshly ground pepper

Pinch of sea salt

2 star anise pods

1 firm medium pear, cubed

1 medium apple, cubed

½ cup each dried apricots and dried figs

¼ cup dried cherries

2 tablespoons brandy

1 tablespoon fresh lemon juice

In a large heavy saucepan combine the water, wine, sugar, lemon and orange zest, spices, and salt. Bring to a boil over medium heat, stirring to dissolve the sugar. Reduce the heat; add the fruits and simmer about 10 minutes, until the pears and apples are tender but still hold their shape, and the dried fruits are plump.

With a slotted spoon transfer the poached fruits to a bowl and set aside. Reduce the poaching liquid over high heat until syrupy and reduced by half, about 10 minutes or so, making sure the star anise and cinnamon sticks are left behind.

Take off the heat, stir in the brandy and lemon juice, then strain right into the bowl with the poached fruits. Stir gently to combine. Cool until barely warm before spooning over the panna cotta (see recipe, page 161), or cover and refrigerate to store until ready to serve.

LEMON PANNA COTTA

2 tablespoons brandy

4 tablespoons water

3 teaspoons unflavored gelatin

3 cups heavy cream

1 cup sugar

⅛ teaspoon sea salt

1 cup plain yogurt, nonfat

1 tablespoon lemon zest,
   chopped

Dash of ground cinnamon

Pour the brandy and water into a small bowl, sprinkle the gelatin over and let stand for about 5 minutes to soften the gelatin.

Meanwhile, place the cream, sugar, and salt into a heavy medium-size saucepan over medium heat. Stir until the sugar is dissolved and the mixture is hot. Add the softened gelatin and whisk to dissolve. Whisk in the yogurt, lemon zest, and cinnamon until well blended and smooth.

Ladle or pour the mixture into a large liquid-measuring cup and divide into 8 custard cups or ramekins set on a tray. Loosely cover with plastic wrap and chill the tray of panna cotta cups for 4 hours or up to overnight.

To unmold, loosen by cutting around the edges of each panna cotta. Set each cup in a shallow bowl of hot (not boiling) water for 10 seconds and immediately invert onto a plate. Spoon the slightly warm compote over or around each panna cotta and serve. If you wish, you can skip the unmolding process, and serve the panna cotta right from the ramekins, topping generously with the compote.

GRAPE CROSTATA WITH RICOTTA CREAM

This excellent pastry recipe is one I have made for years from Johanne Killeen and George Germon's *Cucina Simpatica: Robust Trattoria Cooking*, one of my all-time favorite cookbooks. The crostata is a free-form, rustic pie baked on parchment paper, and it's easy to make, even if you're afraid of working with pastry. There's no fitting into pie pans or making a crust look perfect. If it bubbles and spills over, it's even better. Not even a lone crumb will be left behind.

SERVES 8

For the crust

2 cups unbleached white flour

¼ cup granulated sugar

½ teaspoon sea salt

8 ounces (2 sticks) very cold, unsalted butter, cut into pieces

1 large egg

¼ cup ice water

For the filling

½ cup sweet orange marmalade

2 pounds seedless grapes, washed and halved

2 tablespoons brown sugar

1 tablespoon cornstarch

2 tablespoons butter, unsalted

2 tablespoons water

2 tablespoons granulated sugar

In a food processor, combine the flour with the sugar and salt. Add the cold butter and egg and pulse 5 times until the mixture is crumbly. Add 1–2 tablespoons ice water at a time, or more as needed, and pulse again until a dough ball has formed. Remove and flatten the dough, wrap and chill for 30 minutes. (This will make it easier to roll out.) On a clean work surface liberally sprinkled with flour, begin to roll out the pastry to a 12-inch-wide and ¼-inch-thick circle. Using a rolling pin, apply light pressure while rolling outward from the center of the dough. Every once in awhile, you may need to flour your pin and also gently lift under the dough with your fingers, adding more flour to make sure it isn't sticking. Also, turn the pastry a quarter turn so it rolls out uniformly. As the edges fray, pinch them with your finger and continue rolling. Lift the pastry and put onto a large parchment paper-lined baking pan. It's important to put your pastry on the baking pan before filling.

Preheat the oven to 400°F. Spread the marmalade over the pastry base leaving a 3-inch edge around the outside of the circle. Toss the grapes with the brown sugar and cornstarch, then spread the grapes all over the base, piling them toward the center, and dot with the butter. Fold in the sides of the pastry toward the center leaving the center uncovered, pinching the pastry to form a circle. Use a pastry brush to dab water all over the top edge of the pastry and sprinkle the pastry with the granulated sugar. Bake in the preheated oven for 30–40 minutes, until the pastry edges are golden brown. Allow to cool for 10 minutes. Cut into wedges and serve warm with dollops of chilled ricotta cream (see recipe, page 163).

RICOTTA CREAM

1 cup ricotta cheese

2 tablespoons heavy cream

2 tablespoons honey

1 teaspoon orange zest

Mix the ricotta cheese with the heavy cream, honey, and orange zest. (Use fresh ricotta from page 65 that has drained for 20 minutes.)

PAN-ROASTED PEACHES WITH LAVENDER AND ROSEMARY

You can never have enough dessert recipes, especially during midsummer, when peaches are at their peak. I have taken one of my favorite methods of cooking—pan roasting—and used this technique to create this heavenly dessert, revealing gorgeous roasted peaches, shimmering with caramelized fruit juices. Other seasonal fruit, like nectarines and pears, also work well. Make a good thing even better and accent the caramel notes of the peaches by finishing these off with homemade salted caramel sauce dripped over vanilla ice cream, or a spoonful of creamy mascarpone cheese.

SERVES 6

2 tablespoons dried lavender

1 tablespoon fresh rosemary, chopped fine

1 cup organic sugar

Pinch of sea salt

3 firm peaches, cut in half and pitted

3 tablespoons unsalted butter

Dulce de leche (salted caramel sauce, see page 167)

Vanila ice cream or mascarpone cheese

In a food processor, make the lavender and rosemary-infused sugar. Process the herbs first for about 30 seconds, then add the sugar and a pinch of salt and blend until well incorporated. You can also crush and grind the herbs with a mortar and pestle, then blend with the sugar in a small bowl.

To pan roast the peaches, first liberally sprinkle cut sides of the halved peaches with the infused sugar. (Store any remaining infused sugar in a covered jar for other uses; it's wonderful sprinkled over fresh summer fruit or as a sweetener for hot or iced teas.)

Heat a cast iron skillet over medium-high heat and melt the butter in the hot pan. Once the butter has melted, arrange the peaches in the skillet, cut side down. Cook for 3–5 minutes without disturbing the fruit, until the cut sides begin to brown. Reduce the heat to low and continue to pan roast for another 5 minutes or until tender. Flip the peaches and baste with the butter and caramelized juices. The total cooking time will depend on the ripeness of your peaches; firm peaches are better for this recipe than super soft ones. Transfer the peaches to serving dishes, drizzle the caramel sauce over the roasted peaches, serving extra sauce on the side.

Dollop some ice cream or mascarpone cheese on top and serve immediately.

DULCE DE LECHE (SALTED CARAMEL SAUCE)

When I first visited Argentina, I immediately became a big fan of dulce de leche. Everywhere we looked, there was dulce de leche. From pastries, snacks and ice cream, to other desserts, we were never far from this sweet treat. This homemade caramel sauce is delicious, quick, and easy to make at home, and so much better than the store-bought varieties. The hard part is not eating it all in one sitting!

MAKES 1 CUP

1 cup granulated sugar

6 tablespoons unsalted butter, cut up into 6 pieces

½ cup heavy cream

1 teaspoon pure vanilla extract

1 teaspoon coarse sea salt

Heat the sugar in a saucepan over medium heat until liquefied and amber in color, stirring with a wooden spoon. Once the sugar is completely melted, add the butter and stir until dissolved. Slowly add in the heavy cream—it tends to bubble up—and heat for one minute.

Remove from heat and stir in the vanilla extract and sea salt. Cool and store in an airtight Mason jar. The sauce will keep for up to two weeks in the refrigerator.

FARM STAND FRUIT CRISP

Fresh fruit always makes an appealing finish to any meal. Turn your next meal into something special by finishing it with this uncomplicated, crumbly oat and almond crisp, using your favorite farm stand fruit.

SERVES 6

For the fruit filling

2 pounds fresh fruit (berries or pitted stone fruit)

½ cup granulated sugar

1 tablespoon cornstarch

1 tablespoon lemon juice

¼ teaspoon sea salt

For the oat streusel topping

½ cup rolled oats

¾ cup almond flour

3 tablespoons unbleached white flour

½ cup firmly packed light brown sugar

8 tablespoons (1 stick) unsalted butter, room temperature

½ teaspoon cardamom or nutmeg

To finish

Heavy cream or ice cream

Wash and prepare the fruit as needed. Berries are fine as is, but whole fruits like peaches, apricots, cherries, or strawberries need some love—remove the pits from cherries, trim and cut the strawberries, and slice peaches into chunks. For best results, try to slice the fruit into evenly sized pieces, which will result in more even cooking.

In a large bowl, mix the sugar and cornstarch, then add the fruit, lemon juice, and salt, and toss until well combined. Preheat the oven to 325°F.

For the oat streusel topping, mix all the ingredients together in a small bowl until well combined. Set aside. Pour the fruit mixture into your baking dish of choice and cover with the oat streusel topping.

Bake for 35–40 minutes. Cooking times will vary from oven to oven. You'll know the crisp is finished baking when the edges begin to bubble and the topping is golden brown.

Spoon into bowls and serve warm with heavy cream or your favorite ice cream.

chef's tip
Mixing the sugar and cornstarch together in the mixing bowl before adding the fruit helps distribute the cornstarch and prevents any clumping.

GRAPE GRANOLA BARS

I really love granola bars, especially when I am feeling fatigued and longing for a quick pick-me-up snack. Who can resist the combination of crunchy homemade granola bars and sweet grape jelly? These delicious energy bars will boost your mood in seconds!

MAKES 1 DOZEN

2 ½ cups ready-to-eat granola, divided

3 cups flour, divided

½ teaspoon baking soda

½ teaspoon sea salt

8 ounces (2 sticks) unsalted butter, plus extra for pan

1 cup powdered sugar

1 large egg

1 egg yolk

1 (10-ounce) jar grape jelly

Heat the oven to 375°F. Brush a 13 x 9 x 2-inch baking dish with butter or use a nonstick cooking spray.

In a food processor, finely crush 1 ½ cups of the granola. Transfer to a medium mixing bowl and stir in 2 ½ cups flour, the baking soda, and salt to the crushed granola.

In a large mixing bowl, beat the butter and sugar until smooth. Add the whole egg and yolk, beating until well-blended. Stir in the granola-flour mixture—the dough will be stiff.

Set aside about ¾ cup of the dough. Press the remaining dough into the bottom of the pan.

Bake the crust for 10 minutes.

Meanwhile, combine the remaining 1 cup granola and ½ cup flour with the ¾ cup reserved dough, stir well and break into loose crumbs. Stir the jelly in a small bowl to loosen it up for spreading.

Remove the baked crust from the oven and spread with the grape jelly. With your fingers, crumble the remaining dough over the jelly layer. Put back in the oven and bake for about 20 minutes or until golden brown.

Cool completely before cutting into bars.

MULLED RED WINE ICE CREAM

Ring in the holiday season and the colder months with a pot of mulled wine infused with floral and fruity flavors from exotic whole spices, orange, and brandy. Making a batch of mulled wine is very warming and comforting. Adding some love by stirring a mulled wine syrup into this ice cream base is even better! This flavorful treat will spice up any family celebration or holiday gathering.

MAKES 1 QUART

2 teaspoons whole coriander seed

6 whole allspice berries

4 cardamom pods, lightly crushed

1 (4-inch) cinnamon stick

2 star anise pods

2 teaspoons pink peppercorns

1 bottle (750 ml) Cabernet Sauvignon

½ cup port wine

1 orange, sliced thin

6 egg yolks

¾ cup sugar

2 cups heavy cream

1 cup whole milk

3 tablespoons brandy

½ teaspoon sea salt

In a dry skillet over high heat, toast the spices for about one minute, stirring frequently, until they are fragrant.

In a medium saucepan over medium heat bring the Cabernet, port, and toasted spices to a simmer. Squeeze the juice of 1 orange through a strainer to catch any seeds, then slice up the orange and add to the pan. Cook, stirring occasionally, reducing the wine to ⅓ cup of thick syrup. Strain out the spices and bits of orange and set aside to cool.

In another clean medium saucepan, whisk together the egg yolks and sugar until well-combined and slightly thickened. Whisk in the heavy cream and milk until fully incorporated, add the mulled wine syrup, and cook over medium heat, stirring with a wooden spoon until a custard forms. You will know it's thick enough when a finger swiped across the back of the spoon leaves a clean line. Stir in the brandy and salt, then pour the custard through a fine strainer into a container. Chill in the refrigerator for at least 2 hours.

Once the custard is chilled, churn it in an ice cream maker according to the manufacturer's instructions. Transfer the ice cream to the freezer and let harden for at least 4 hours before serving.

SANTA BARBARA COUNTY WINERIES

Aether
Alexander & Wayne
Alma Rosa
Alta Maria
Ampelos
Andrew Murray
Arthur Earl
Artiste
Au Bon Climat
Babcock
Baehner Fournier
Beckmen
Bedford
Bernat
Bien Nacido
Blackjack
Blair Fox
Brander
Brewer-Clifton
Bridlewood
Brophy Clark
Buscador
Buttonwood
Byron
Ca' Del Grevino
Cambria

Carhartt
Carina
Carivintas
Carr
Casa Cassara
Casa Dumetz
Cebada
CCGP
Cinque Stelle
Challen
Clos Pepe
Coldheaven
Consilience
Coquelicot
Costa de Oro
Cottonwood Canyon
Crawford
Crown Point
Dascomb
Demetria
Dierberg
Dreamcôte
Dragonette
DV8
Epiphany
Ferguson Crest

Fess Parker
Fiddlehead
Firestone
Flying Goat
Foley
Foxen
Frequency
Gainey
Grassini
Grimm's Bluff
Gypsy Canyon
Happy Canyon
Hilliard Bruce
Hitching Post
Holus Bolus
Imagine
J Ludlow
J.Wilkes
Jaffurs
Jalama
Jamie Slone
JCR
Kaena
Kalyra
Ken Brown

Kenneth Volk
Kita
Koehler
Lafond
La Fenetre
LaMontagne
Larner
Lavender Oak
Lieu Dit
LinCourt
Lions Peak
Longoria
Lucas & Lewellen
Lucky Dogg
Lumen
Lutum
Margerum
Martian
Melville
Montemar
Mosby
Municipal
  Winemakers
Pali

WINERY, VINEYARDS, OR CELLAR: WHAT'S THE DIFFERENCE?

Palmina
Pence
Presidio
Presqu'ile
Qupé
Rancho Sisquoc
Refugio Ranch
Rideau
Riverbench
Roblar
Royal Oaks
Runway
Rusack
Saarloos & Sons
SAMsARA
Sandhi
Sanford
Sanger
Santa Barbara
Section
Sevtap
Silver

Solminer
Spear
Stolpman
Summerland
Sunstone
Sweetzer
Tensley
The Valley Project
Thorne
Timbre
Toccata
Toretti
Trancend
Tres Hermanas
Turiya
Vincent
Vogelzang
Westerly
Whitcraft
Zaca Mesa
Zotovich

Winery: A bonded winery is a licensed building or property that produces wine. For example, you may ask to visit a winery or tasting room. Some produce wine—but don't have a winery on site. Some have permits for tasting rooms while others do not.

Vineyards: A vineyard is a plantation of grape-bearing vines grown for wine making. You can have a vineyard without having a winery—grapegrowers may sell their grapes to other wineries to be used in wine under a different label, or they may produce their own label by taking their grapes to a bonded/licensed winery and use their equipment and facilities to produce the finished wine.

Cellar: A wine cellar by definition is a place to store and age wine. These can be as basic as a temperature-controlled warehouse or as elaborate as a cave dug deep into the hill and naturally cooled by the earth. Sometimes, you will see "cellar" used as part of the name of the wine.

RESOURCE GUIDE

For inspiration, decor and information:

Bernscott Pottery
www.bernscottpottery.com
Hand-thrown, high-fired
earthenware cookware,
tableware and tiles in
Ojai, California

B.Living
www.blivingstore.com
Vintage items for modern life,
an online store in Santa Ynez,
California

Cailloux Cheese Shop
www.caillouxcheeseshop.com
Upscale European-style
specialty food store
in Solvang, California

FOLD Santa Barbara
www.foldsantabarbara.com
Handcrafted table and
kitchen linens, napkins, dish
towels, and tea towels in
Santa Barbara, California

Global Eye Art Collective
www.geartco.com
Creative and practical
one-of-a-kind handmade
ceramics, paintings and
jewelry in Santa Ynez,
California

Porch Santa Barbara
www.porchsb.com
Home & garden shop
showcasing the indoor/
outdoor lifestyle in
Carpinteria, California

Red Hen Cannery
www.redhencannery.com
Artisanal, small-batch jam
company, using family
recipes, fruits, and herbs from
family farms on the Central
Coast, based in Carpinteria,
California

**Santa Barbara Vintners
Association**
www.sbcountywines.com
A nonprofit organization
founded to support and
promote Santa Barbara
County authentic wine
producing and the wine
grape growing region, with
festivals, wine country
weekends, educational
seminars, and tastings

**Solvang Conference &
Visitors Bureau (SCVB)**
www.solvangusa.com
Official guide for visiting
Solvang, California

Tenley Fohl Photography
www.tenleyfohlphotography.com
Wine country lifestyle
photography of California's
Central Coast region in the
Santa Ynez Valley, California

Visit the Santa Ynez Valley
www.visitsyv.com
Everything you need to know
about the Santa Ynez Valley

index

index

index

Acknowledgments

I planned to write this cookbook, after self-publishing my first two titles, because I wanted to share recipes inspired by the third region in which I regularly work—the *Wine Country* in Santa Ynez Valley, on California's Central Coast.

The amazing feat of producing this book came about quite quickly after contacting, and eventually partnering, with my new publisher, M27 Editions. Thank you to everyone at Media 27: Shukri Farhad, Susan Noble, Mike Verbois, Ruth Verbois, Scott Moseley, Stephen Ensminger, and, especially, Judi Muller. I could not have done this without your calm, professional demeanor, *and* patience. I am immensely grateful to all of you for recognizing my abilities as a chef and author, and I value your sincere and enthusiastic encouragement for my vision.

This book would remain only a dream without the loving support of my family, my friends, and all those who continue to believe in me and my work. To the many for whom I've had the pleasure of preparing meals, there is nothing more gratifying than receiving your compliments—you are an endless source of inspiration for me.

It was an amazing experience working with photographer Tenley Fohl. You brilliantly captured everything that I set on the table. Your love of Wine Country is so clear in the way your photography invokes emotion and sense of place.

Great appreciation is due to my recipe editor, Kamila Storr. Knowing just how dedicated you are to the preparation of food and cooking is always a great comfort to me.

To Joan Tapper, with your expert editing and advice you truly transformed the manuscript from good to *outstanding*—thank you!

My sincere thanks to Jen Weers for your attention to detail in creating the index for this, my third book—your organizing skills are nothing short of amazing!

A huge thanks to the entire team at Beckmen Vineyards, and to Jim Clendenen of Au Bon Climat for providing the Santa Ynez Valley winery venues for the photo production of this book. Being surrounded by vines was (awe) inspiring.

I'm always thrilled to visit with local wine consultant Jessica Garver of The Monk's Table. You are a fount of knowledge and sage advice, and always open to sharing your wine discoveries.

Many thanks, as well, to Karen from B.Living, Kristen from Global Eye Art Collective, Karen from Bernscott Pottery, and Viktoriya from FOLD Santa Barbara. Your handmade wares, vintage collectibles, and beautifully hand-sewn linens *made* the photographs in this book.

Thanks to Janelle from Cailloux Cheese—the best cheeses ever!

A special note of thanks to my friend Maureen Foley, who so graciously shared her delicious, award-winning marmalade recipe with me.

I am extremely grateful for the food preparation and styling assistance by my good friends and fellow food professionals Carrie Clough and Danica Dahm. Thank you for your generosity, energy, and positive attitudes—you made the photo productions flow effortlessly!

My deepest thanks and gratitude to all! ♥

"Wine makes every meal an
occasion, every table more elegant,
every day more civilized."

—ANDRÉ SIMON
(1877–1970)